Save A Marriage
Save Our Nation

A Guide to Domestic Tranquility

D. James Kennedy

CORAL RIDGE
MINISTRIES

Published by Coral Ridge Ministries
Printed in the United States of America

ISBN 1-929626-18-5

Coral Ridge Ministries
P.O. Box 40
Fort Lauderdale, FL 33308

1.800.988.7884
letters@coralridge.org
www.coralridge.org

Contents

Introduction

Part One Save A Marriage

One   Capturing The Bird Of Paradise 11

Two   Why People Get Married 19

Three   The Essence Of Marriage 27

Four   Sand In Your Shoes? 41

Five   Making Marriage Work 53

Six   Mistakes Husbands Often Make 65

Seven   When You Are Going In Different Directions 75

Eight   Principles For A Successful Marriage 87

Part Two Save Our Nation

Nine   The Importance Of Marriage 103

Ten   Turning The Tide 113

Eleven   Reasons To Reject Same-Sex Marriage 125

Marriage Matters

Marriage is a good thing. In fact, it's a very good thing. Far more than a personal preference, marriage is God's idea for the happiness, health, and well-being of men, women, children, and cultures.

When God said in Genesis, "It is not good that man should be alone," He was making a statement fully supported by social science research. Thirteen top scholars on family life assessed decades of research and collaborated in a 2002 joint report that reached 21 conclusions about the importance of marriage. Their definitive report, *Why Marriage Matters*, found that marriage has enormous financial, emotional, and health consequences for men, women, children, and society. Among the report's conclusions were findings that:

- Children of divorce are less likely to graduate from college and achieve high-status jobs.
- Children in two-parent homes are healthier, on average, than children who do not live with mom and dad.
- When parents divorce, they double the odds that their children, when adults, will end up divorced.
- Married men earn between 10 to 40 percent more than single men with similar education and job histories.

- Married people, especially married men, have longer life expectancies than otherwise similar singles.
- Poverty rates are higher for women who divorce or have children outside marriage. Between 20 and 30 percent of women who divorce will end up in poverty.
- Married mothers are less likely to experience depression than mothers who are single or who live with a man.
- Domestic violence is less likely among married women than among women who live with a man or who are dating. People who live together are three times more likely to report violent arguments than married people.
- Marriage reduces the risk of crime. Single and divorced women are four to five times more likely to be victims of violent crime in any given year than married women. Boys raised in single-parent homes are about twice as likely (and boys raised in stepfamilies three times as likely) to have committed a crime that leads to incarceration by the time they reach their early thirties, even after controlling for factors such as race, mother's education, neighborhood quality, and cognitive ability.

Not only does social science attest to the benefits of marriage, but history does too. Harvard historian Carle Zimmerman examined the breakdown of the cultures of Greece and Rome in his *Last State of Disintegration*, written in 1947. Many of the cultural indicators relating to marriage and the family that he found present in ancient

Greece and Rome are also in evidence in American culture today. Zimmerman found that these two cultures in collapse had the following characteristics:

- Marriage was not held sacred, and divorce was a frequent occurrence.
- The primacy of marriage was lost. In its place, alternative forms of marriage came into favor.
- Feminist movements abounded.
- Public disrespect for parents and authority, in general, increased.
- Juvenile delinquency, promiscuity, and rebellion grew more common.
- Married couples grew less likely to accept family responsibilities and have children.
- Adultery grew in acceptance and became more common.
- Tolerance for sexual perversion—especially homosexuality.

The evidence from both social science and history shows that marriage matters for all of us. Not only do men and women benefit when married, but children thrive in homes with both mom and dad. And society reaps benefits, too. That is because the family is the fundamental social unit—the building block on which any culture is built. Healthy families mean a healthy culture. Likewise, when the marriage bond is frayed or broken, the larger culture pays a price.

Our culture is now paying that price. Marriage is now under attack in the culture, in the courts, and in the legislatures of America. Our nation not only has the highest divorce rate in the world, but roughly one-third of all births in the U.S. are to unmarried women. More than half of all American children will spend at least a significant portion of their childhood in a one-parent home before they reach eighteen. And now another attack is being waged against marriage, as homosexual activists attempt to use the courts to redefine marriage as the union of two men or two women. This assault on marriage is placing our homes and our nation at risk.

Save A Marriage, Save Our Nation offers you practical help to protect and strengthen your own marriage and highlights the critical importance of marriage and family to our nation. In addition, I have included a brief overview of the reasons why homosexual marriage is detrimental to the health of marriage in our nation.

It is my prayer that this book will inform and equip you to make your marriage the very best it can be—and, in so doing, it will strengthen, perhaps preserve, our nation.

May God's richest blessings rest on your home and on our land.

D. James Kennedy, Ph.D.

Part One

Save A Marriage

One

Capturing The Bird Of Paradise

On a recent television program, a handsome young man was talking to an older man about whether or not he should get married. After a number of comments concerning the young lady in question, the older man finally asked, "Do you love her?"

The young man replied, "Oh, yes! I'm madly in love with her."

"Then by all means, marry her," said the older man.

Most people conceive of love as a feeling that is like a mysterious bird of paradise. We do not know where it comes from, why it comes to some, or why it leaves others. But somehow this mysterious bird flaps its wings, floats down on two people, and they are "in love." What a glorious, marvelous experience!

When two people "fall in love," they often get married. Then two years later, they wake up one morning and decide the bird has flown away and taken paradise with it. No one knows why, but the bird has gone, and the once-happy couple has "fallen out of love." So they get divorced and wander through life, waiting and hoping that the mysterious bird will descend from the skies and once again bring them a touch of paradise.

This secular view of marriage has created devastating consequences. Statistics indicate that one out of two marriages in America ends in divorce. That means the chances of remaining in paradise are only fifty-fifty—very discouraging odds for any venture, much less one that can leave permanent scars and a long trail of heartache.

I read in a magazine about a Hollywood actress who was getting married because she was in love. This time she believed it was going to work because she was really in love. The other three times she thought she was in love, but she had been wrong. This time she was sure.

This flaky view of romantic love has penetrated the Church to an alarming degree, and the result is an increasing number of divorces among Christians. I have counseled young couples who, before they were married, boldly professed their love and made assertions of an undying concern for one another. After two years of marriage, I have seen them axing one another to death in a divorce court. What happened to the undying love that was going to last until the stars burned out and the mountains fell into the sea?

Romantic Love

Most people would say that love and romance are the foundation of any successful marriage. This is a beautiful sentiment, but it is not true. In fact, many marital problems result from an erroneous concept of what love is.

Dr. John W. Drakeford, in his book, *How to Keep A Good Thing Going*, describes the characteristics of romantic love. He says that being in love is preeminently an experience of the emotions that causes irrational behavior and often immobilizes its victims. No wonder so many marriages fail.

Some of the confusion about love comes from the

different ways the word is used in the English language. "I love my new Honda." "I love baseball." "I love your hairdo." "I love chocolate."

Remember the song that says, "What the world needs now is love, sweet love"? The world quickly adopted the songwriter's ideas, and now we have more "free love" than ever before—or free sex, as it should be called. Many people use the word "love" when they really mean lust or sex.

The word love is also used to describe the feeling of infatuation or what we call "puppy love"—so named because it lasts about as long as a puppy remains a puppy. Unfortunately, many couples get married on the basis of infatuation and then wonder why their love doesn't last until the puppy is grown. "Infatuation" comes from the Latin word *infatuate*, whose root meaning also forms the English word "foolish." Anyone who builds a relationship, especially their marriage, on infatuation is foolish indeed.

When I was a teenager, I often sang these words from a popular song: "Will I ever find the girl on my mind, the one who is my ideal? Or will I pass her by and never even know that she was my ideal?" Today, I'm wise enough to know—that is a bunch of hogwash! Many single people delude themselves into thinking that if they find that one soul mate—Mr. or Miss Right—they will experience the pitter-patter in their heart, hear the flip-flap of the bird of paradise, and sail off into the sunset.

Reality, however, is a different scenario. When one spouse or the other loses the feeling of love, the bird falls like a dead owl, and someone is left out on a limb all alone.

Learning to Love

This feeling that people call love is not what the Bible means by love at all. According to Scripture, love is not a feeling; love is a way of acting. True love, as God's Word tells us, is a way of treating other people. Notice in the following Scripture passage that there is not one tinge of emotion—not even a palpitation!

> *Love is patient, love is kind. It does not envy, it does not boast, it is not proud. It is not rude, it is not self-seeking, it is not easily angered, it keeps no record of wrongs. Love does not delight in evil but rejoices with the truth. It always protects, always trusts, always hopes, always perseveres (1 Corinthians 13:4-7 NIV).*

When a young man and woman are dating, they are extremely patient and kind with one another. They never say anything rude or demand their own way. Angry words and actions are seldom exhibited. They defend each other and trust one another implicitly. What happens, then, when these same two people get married? Why do their actions change?

For thousands of years (and in some eastern countries today), the majority of marriages were arranged by parents. The young people involved sometimes never saw each other until their wedding day.

A young lady from India was to be married to a young man whom she had never met. One day she received a letter from her fiancé in which he tried to begin a relationship and get acquainted prior to the wedding. The young woman, however, returned the letter unopened, saying she believed love should be developed after marriage and not before. In explaining her view, this young Indian woman said, "When we are born, we cannot choose who will be our mother and father, or our brothers and sisters. Yet we learn to live with them and to love them. So it is with our husband or wife."

In societies where this philosophy is accepted, divorce is almost nonexistent. I am not suggesting we go back to the practice of arranged marriages, but I am saying that romantic love has little to do with a successful marriage relationship.

If two complete strangers meet and treat one another according to 1 Corinthians 13, after a while the feeling of love will also come. On the other hand, no matter how crazy head-over-heels in love you have fallen with someone, if he or she violates the love principles in God's Word, romantic love will fly out the window—and so will the feeling.

Love, according to the Bible's definition, involves two aspects: doing and enduring. We can understand this better by looking at Jesus Christ. The life of Christ is divided by theologians into two parts: His active obedience and His passive obedience.

The active obedience of Jesus was everything He did: Jesus went about doing good. He healed the sick, He fed the hungry, He forgave the sinner, and He comforted the mourner. Christ's passive obedience (from which we get the word passion) involves the things He endured: mockery, insults, betrayal, injustice, emotional turmoil, sorrow, physical pain, separation from His heavenly Father. Jesus Christ was the perfect embodiment of love as it is defined in 1 Corinthians 13. Doing good and enduring evil—that is what love is all about.

A Rose by Any Other Name

Some time ago a lady came to me and said, "I don't love my husband anymore, and I haven't loved him for a long time. There is no love in our home. I think we should get a divorce."

"I am sorry to hear that," I replied. "Tell me about it. Did you ever love him?"

"Oh, yes. When I married him, I loved him very much. He was so kind and considerate. But after we were married, he became indifferent toward me. Then he started treating me badly and saying nasty things to me, until I lost all love for him." She paused a moment and then continued, "You know, some years ago I was very sick and had an operation. While I was in the hospital, my husband brought me flowers and candy, sat on the bed, held my hand, and read to me. It's the strangest thing, but I began to love him again at that time."

"Oh, really?" I asked.

"Yes, but it didn't last. After I got out of the hospital, it wasn't long before he was ignoring me again. I haven't felt any love for him in years. So there's nothing left to do. Don't you agree that I should get a divorce?"

"I'll tell you what the Bible says you should do. If you don't love your husband, if you haven't loved him for years, then you should go home, get down on your knees, repent of your sin, and ask the Lord and your husband to forgive you."

She didn't reply, but I've never seen a more shocked expression on anyone's face!

Love isn't an "I hope so" or "I wish I could" or "Maybe I will." Love is a command. "See that ye love one another with a pure heart fervently" (1 Peter 1:22). "He has given us this command: Whoever loves God must also love his brother" (1 John 4:21 NIV).

If you don't love your husband or wife, you are disobeying God, and you need to repent of that sin. "But how can I love him (or her) when I don't feel like it?" You can't command a feeling, but you can command your mouth to speak lovingly to your spouse, you can make your hands touch with tenderness, and you can decide to be patient and kind.

If I were to say, "A rose is a delightful aroma, a lovely fragrance." You would say, "No, that is not quite right. A rose is a flower, and it produces a fragrance. But the aroma isn't the flower." When we do what 1 Corinthians 13 says, one of the by-products is the feeling that people call love—the fragrance. But the love—the real rose—is what we do and what we endure for one another.

Love—like a rose—is very delicate and needs to be handled gently. Anyone who has ever had a rose garden knows that beautiful flowers do not happen naturally. Roses require a great deal of work and attention. You can keep the fragrance in your marriage by carefully nourishing and caring for the love that is there. How about your marriage? Has the once sweet-smelling rose turned brown around the edges and lost not only its fragrance, but also its beauty?

The love the Bible talks about doesn't come naturally for fallen man. Because of our selfish, sinful nature, we do not have it within us to love. Love is supernatural: "God is love" (1 John 4:8, 16).

How, then, can we ever experience love? God has given us the Holy Spirit, and one of the fruits of the Spirit is love. (See Galatians 5:22.) If you try to love your husband or wife, but ignore God—the fountain and source of all love—you will find yourself chasing an illusive rainbow. If, however, you seek God with all your heart and ask Him to fill you with His Spirit of love, a miracle will occur in your heart and in your marriage.

Heavenly Father, teach us how to love one another. Forgive us for our misconceptions and ignorance about what love really is. By the power of Your Holy Spirit, help us to love our spouses with the love of Jesus and by the principles established in Your Word. In Jesus' name. Amen.

Two

Why People Get Married

Why do people get married? To have someone to take care of them? To legalize their living arrangement? To have children and a family? For security and companionship in their old age?

If you observed the habits and conduct of many American marriages, you would conclude that one of these ideas must be the reason behind this institution. But what is God's purpose in having two people marry?

Long before God established the Church, the state, or the school, He created marriage. The goal for this God-ordained institution is clearly set forth for us in Scripture. First mentioned in Genesis, it is later repeated several times in the New Testament: "They shall be one." (See Genesis 2:24; Matthew 19:6; Mark 10:8.)

Oneness is God's purpose for marriage, yet most of us have only dimly perceived the supreme goal God intends for a husband and wife to achieve. In fact, most couples do not have any concept of what they are trying to accomplish in their marriage.

The oneness designed for marriage partners is compared to the relationship believers share with Christ. In this "mystical union," Christ, the Bridegroom, joins Himself to His bride, the Church; and they become one. In this oneness with Christ, man enjoys his highest spiritual communion. On earth, God intends for us to enjoy a similar union in marriage. (See Ephesians 5:23–33.)

Some people say that marriage is a fifty-fifty partnership. Others say, "No, it is not fifty-fifty; it is a 100 percent partnership." According to Christ, marriage is not a partnership at all; it is a relationship. Marriage is the closest relationship any two people can know in this world. Even the relationship between parent and child does not involve the same kind of oneness that a husband and wife enjoy.

God's Purpose for Marriage

To understand God's original purpose for marriage, we must go back to the Garden of Eden. God placed Adam in that perfect environment and provided for his every possible need. Anything he desired was available to him for the taking; he simply had to pluck it off a tree. This man whom God created was the epitome of humanity—physically perfect and with a superior intellect.

Yet, when God looked upon Adam—with his tremendous mental capacities, his physical prowess, his perfect environment, his spiritual communion with the Creator—He found man lacking. God said, "It is not good that the man should be alone" (Genesis 2:18).

The singles movement in America today says, "God, You are wrong. It is good for man to be alone. It's really cool!" Even married people accept the current fads of modern society and go their own way, never realizing that the deepest, most fulfilling spiritual union that can be experienced with another human being is found in marriage.

Although Adam enjoyed the companionship of

beautiful horses, lovable lions, and cuddly lambs, he did not have a suitable helper. None of the animals could meet Adam's needs, so the Creator designed a completely new being for man. God put Adam into a deep sleep, took one of his ribs, and out of that rib built a woman. The writer of Genesis did not use the word create or fashion, as he had previously, but he wrote that God built a woman.

How did Adam respond when God presented this new created being to him? "'This is it!' Adam exclaimed. 'She is part of my own bone and flesh! Her name is "woman" because she was taken out of man'" (Genesis 2:23 TLB). Adam and Eve enjoyed a perfect oneness that no other couple will ever experience. They were literally one flesh made from the same body.

God designated this oneness when He "called their name Adam" (Genesis 5:2). This concept is contrary to the modern thinking of the liberated woman who wants to maintain her independence. She balks at being called the "Adamses" and instead, keeps her maiden name to prove she is a separate individual.

When a man and woman get married, they are no longer two but one flesh. Although they are not made from the same body, as Adam and Eve were, there is a unique oneness between husband and wife that no other human relationship enjoys. Husbands, your wife is you! Wives, your husband is you! If you can grasp this fact and hold on to it, your marriage will never be the same.

Cutting Off Your Head

God said that a husband and wife are indissolubly one—one flesh. Could you rip off your arm or tear off your leg? No wonder God said He hates divorce. Divorce violently wrenches apart that which is meant to be inseparable. "What therefore God hath joined together, let not man put asunder" (Matthew 19:6).

When you get a cold and have a runny nose, watery eyes, and ringing ears, you try many remedies in an effort to alleviate your suffering. But one solution is never contemplated—cutting off your head! The Bible says the husband is the head of the household. Wives, you may have trouble with your husband, and he may be doing things that displease you, but the answer is not to cut off your head. Husbands, if you are having problems in your marriage, the solution is not to cut out your heart—the wife who loves you.

Once couples realize that the husband/wife relationship is permanent, solutions other than cutting off the undesirable partner will be considered. Most of the problems in marriage start because couples regard their relationship as some sort of probationary experiment that, if it works out, fine; if not, that's too bad—"We tried." They view marriage as a temporary arrangement with a ninety-day, money-back guarantee: 'til the divorce court doth us part; 'til the midlife crisis doth us part. God, however, designed marriage to be a permanent relationship—'til death do you part.

Married couples need to commit themselves to fulfilling the vows they made on their wedding day. The Bible says it is a grievous and heinous sin to break a vow, and God is greatly displeased with those who do so. "When you make a vow to God, do not delay in fulfilling it. He has no pleasure in fools; fulfill your vow" (Ecclesiastes 5:4 NIV). We need to have this same attitude toward our marriage vows. Divorce is not a viable option to marital problems. Commit yourself to the permanence of your marriage, and don't even mention the word divorce in your home.

Marriage is built on commitment—"for better or worse, in sickness and in health." When a man and woman commit themselves for life to one another, they will not have a footnote in the back of their mind that says, "If things get really tough, I'll check out."

Husbands and wives who do not see their marriage as an irrevocable, indissoluble, and permanent union will never experience the oneness that Christ says exists in that special relationship. You may be thinking that this means you are condemned to a life-sentence of misery and heartache. "Oh, he'll never change. He's just like his father." Or, "She'll never be any different. She's just like her mother."

Yet the whole thrust of the biblical message is that God can change people. When we take the position that our spouse will never change, we are insulting God and His Word. By the power of the Holy Spirit, your spouse can become the husband or wife God wants him or her to be.

God has a plan for improving your marriage. If you commit yourself to discovering how you can implement His perfect will in your marital relationship, your marriage will be a success.

Leaving and Cleaving

The concept of oneness—"They shall be one flesh" (Genesis 2:24)—established in the Garden of Eden was preceded by a rather unusual statement: "Therefore shall a man leave his father and his mother, and shall cleave unto his wife" (Genesis 2:24). What do a person's parents have to do with oneness in marriage?

The wedding ceremony drives a stake into time, dividing a person's life into two periods: the time when one is bound to parents and the time when one is bound to husband or wife. That is why leaving is so important. If a couple is going to have oneness with their spouse, a leaving of the parents must first take place.

Sometimes a young person says, "Yes, forsaking all others, leaving father and mother, I take this one to be my husband or wife." Yet, once married, he is continually looking over his shoulder at mom and dad. How many husbands and wives have endeavored to remake their spouse in the image of dear old dad or wonderful mom? "That is not the way dad carved the turkey," or "That's not how mom made an apple pie." The husband is tied to his mother's apron strings, and the wife wants nothing less than good old dad in a younger form. A husband or wife who cannot break the parent/child bond will have difficulty establishing true oneness with his or her marriage partner.

A marriage starts with leaving, but it develops with cleaving. In Genesis 2:24, the word used for "cleave" refers to the kind of bonding that occurs when two pieces of wood are glued together. Today, it is rare to see couples who exhibit a real cleaving to one another.

I heard a story about a civilian couple who were invited to a military banquet where the husband was to be the keynote speaker. The colonel who had invited them showed the wife where she was to sit. He then began to lead the husband to a seat at the head table. The husband stopped and said, "No, I prefer to sit with my wife."

The colonel replied, "I am sorry, but it is military protocol that you be seated up front."

"I don't care about military protocol. God made us one, and you are trying to separate us. I will sit with my wife." When the people attending the banquet overheard the husband's reply, they stood and applauded.

How is the oneness in your marriage? Do you have two soloists, or do you have a duet? Do you have your own interests, your own friends, your own enjoyments, and your own entertainments? Do you allow the world to pull you apart? Do the two of you go your own ways and occasionally meet at the home refueling center?

If this describes your marriage, then ask God to help you experience the deeper joy, love, and peace that come with true oneness. "And they shall be one" (Genesis 2:24). Make that the goal of your marriage.

This is my prayer for you and your spouse:

Father, may the two in each marriage be made one, even as we have been made one in You through Jesus Christ our Lord. May those who have not known true oneness with Christ reach out the hand of faith and put their trust in Him. May they be cleansed, renewed, and enabled to know the oneness in marriage that You have designed for them to enjoy. May each husband and wife be one flesh in You. In Jesus' name. Amen.

Three

The Essence Of Marriage

A cartoon in *The Wall Street Journal* showed an obviously successful businessman looking over the newspaper at his wife and saying, "I communicate all day long at the office—isn't that enough?" We can imagine what the wife must have said to evoke such a response from her husband. The sad reality of this situation leaves little room for humor. How many wives feel hurt and neglected because communication on their husband's part ends when he walks in the door at night?

Communication is as important in the home as it is at the office—or anywhere else. The sharing of thoughts, dreams, plans, problems, and emotions is essential to oneness in a marital relationship. A well-known marriage counselor says the major complaint made by wives is, "My husband won't communicate with me or listen to me."

Because many couples have never grasped the reality of what marriage is all about, they have experienced little in the way of communication. This is due, in part, to the fact that they see their primary goal in marriage as simply earning a living, making a home, and raising a family. Creating a oneness in their relationship hardly enters their minds.

We've all known marriages where the wife is a chatterbox and the husband is a sphinx. A lot of one-sided talk may take place, but no real communication occurs.

The wife complains that her husband doesn't talk to her, but she fails to understand that he can't get a word in edgewise. He's been trying for thirty years and hasn't succeeded yet! So the husband gives up. When the wife wants his opinion, she'll give it to him. When you want to know what the husband thinks, she'll tell you. I know a marriage like this that recently ended in divorce, and the wife was totally oblivious to the real problem.

Many married couples operate with a competitive attitude that says, "Can you top this?" When the husband comes home in the evening, his wife meets him, saying, "What a day I had! The children drove me absolutely wild. I'm so frazzled I can hardly think straight!" What an opportunity for this husband to sympathize with his wife and her situation.

But his response usually is, "Ha! You think you had trouble today. You should have seen it down at that rat race of an office. I mean to tell you the rats were chewing the tails off each other!"

When openness on the part of one spouse is used as an opportunity for ridiculing, scoffing, criticizing, or faultfinding by the other, any kind of deep communication dries up altogether. Marriages often fail because one mate is unwilling to try to meet the needs of the other. Everyone needs to be appreciated, understood, listened to, and respected.

Many couples, if asked, "What are your spouse's greatest aspirations?" would not be able to answer. They cannot identify one another's goals in life, greatest fears, or deepest needs because they never cared enough to ask.

Levels of Communication

Marriage counselors tell us that the number one problem in marriage is poor communication. "We can never discuss anything without your blowing up or walking out." "Why is it that we can never talk anything out?" "What can we do? It seems so hopeless."

Every couple wants to be able to communicate, but somehow, after trying and trying, they have failed repeatedly. Many have given up altogether and resigned themselves to a humdrum marriage with little meaningful sharing. Yet their hearts yearn for a deeper, richer, more intimate relationship with their spouse.

John Powell wrote an interesting book with this thought-provoking title: *Why Am I Afraid to Tell You Who I Am?* Do you share that fear? Many people find it difficult to express their true feelings. Yet it is in the sharing of hearts that a husband and wife are most deeply joined together. How about your marriage? Are feelings freely shared?

Powell has found that people communicate on one or more of five different levels. See if you can determine the level on which you and your spouse usually communicate.

The lowest level of communication is called cliché conversation. On this safe level, no personal risks are involved. Husbands and wives often have this type of conversation: "Good morning. How did you sleep? Your breakfast is on the table. Will you stop for milk on the way home? By the way, the car needs gas. Have a nice day. See you later." This kind of communication may be good for starters, but some couples never get beyond this point. When they have exhausted their little group of clichés, they are left speechless, and all communication ends.

The next level of communication involves reporting the facts about others. Our conversation centers around what we have read, what other people have said, or what someone else has done. "The boss's wife had an operation yesterday." "Your mother called while you were out." "The weatherman said it's going to rain this afternoon." "Johnny got a B in English." No effort is made to offer an opinion or tell how we feel about these issues or events. Gossip is an example of this low level of sharing.

Risky Business

When we can express our ideas and judgments about issues and events, real communication begins. At last, the soul steps out of its solitary confinement and begins to share, in a very limited way, its existence with another person. As soon as you begin to express what you think about something or tell what you believe, you are exposing a piece of yourself. This can be risky business.

To avoid dangerous ground, some people act like politicians. "Well, what do you think?…That's how I feel about it, too." They don't seem to have any opinions about issues, any beliefs about life, or any new ideas. If they do have opinions, they keep them to themselves. On the other hand, some people are very adept at expressing their judgments and convictions on a broad spectrum of subjects, yet no real communication occurs because it is all one-sided.

A higher level of communication occurs when feelings and emotions are honestly expressed. We are not simply sharing something that may have happened (which is a fact), or what we may think about it (which is an opinion), but how we feel about it—our hopes, anxieties, and joys. Some people will discuss their feelings about the safe areas of life, as long as they don't have to share about things that intimately affect them—like their marriage, their feelings toward their husband or wife, or their attitude toward life.

A missionary couple returned from the foreign field because their marriage was dissolving and their ministry was failing. After discussing all their problems with a counselor, the wife finally blurted out, "I didn't love this man when I married him, and I have never loved him since!" Once these deep, hidden feelings were expressed, the problem areas in their marriage could be dealt with honestly and openly. As a result, the husband and wife developed a beautiful new relationship, and they are back on the mission field, serving and glorifying the Lord.

Overcoming the Risks

Once we are able to share our feelings with our spouse, we are on our way to the highest level of communication. This level requires absolute openness and honesty. Many people, however, find that the risks involved on this very personal level are too great, and they are afraid to venture forth. They have a fear of being rejected or scorned if they bare their souls and share their true feelings. This fear of rejection causes many people to clam up, and feelings go unexpressed. When these emotions are never lovingly brought to the surface where they can be discussed and resolved, they remain locked up inside the person. Like a splinter buried deep in the skin, these feelings fester and can destroy any hope for an intimate relationship between husband and wife.

Other people have a fear of being betrayed. For this reason, openness must always be met with responding loyalty on the part of the listener. Proverbs 31 says of the virtuous wife, "The heart of her husband doth safely trust in her, so that he shall have no need of spoil. She will do him good and not evil all the days of her life" (verses 11–12). The same should be true of a righteous husband. If we are not trustworthy, how can we expect our mates to be honest and open with us? It is crucial to a healthy marriage for partners not to betray the confidences shared with one another.

Openness requires a certain degree of vulnerability, and vulnerability can only exist where there is complete trust. A deep marital relationship is built on open honesty. Wife, how do you feel about your husband? Husband, how do you feel about your wife? Would you dare tell them?

Some husbands and wives who try to be loving often fail to speak the truth to their mates. Real feelings are not expressed because they feel it would hurt their partner, yet any deep personal relationship is based upon complete honesty with one another. Many marriages never progress to a more intimate level of sharing because so much has been left unsaid. If the truth is presented in a loving and positive manner, it will generally be well received.

If you and your mate are willing to deal constructively and honestly with the deepest feelings of your life, one thing is essential—an opportunity. Husbands and wives should plan and schedule time alone together where communication can develop in an uninterrupted atmosphere of peace and quiet. This may seem impossible on a regular basis, but unless you make the opportunity, your quality of communication will remain on the lowest levels. To reach that peak level of deep emotional sharing, you must make an effort to spend quality time alone with your mate.

You may need to rethink your priorities. Which is more important: your job or your wife? The household or your husband? Set aside time to relax and enjoy being together, sharing ideas and activities. Learn to listen sensitively to your mate's innermost thoughts, fears, and feelings. If your husband (or wife) has difficulty expressing himself, then you take the initiative and open up to him first. Soon he will feel free to expose his hopes, dreams, and desires.

The Wall of Ice

Have you ever tried to communicate with someone, only to find yourself talking to a stone wall? As soon as you hit on a sensitive issue or begin sharing on a personal level, the barriers go up and the subject is changed to a less threatening topic. What causes these communication blockers?

One of the most common reasons for blocked communication is resentment. Many times a husband or wife tries to communicate with his or her spouse, but the efforts are blocked by a cold, icy wall of resentment. This wall is built on the memory of some previous hurt, slight, or wound.

Resentment is like an inner thermometer that measures the degree of unforgiveness a person is harboring. Are you a resentful person? If so, then you are not a forgiving person. God's Word says to be "tenderhearted, forgiving one another, even as God for Christ's sake hath forgiven you" (Ephesians 4:32). Once you learn to forgive your spouse, the lines of communication will be unclogged, and times of tender sharing will become more frequent.

Jay Adams, a well-known Christian psychologist, in his book, *Christian Living in the Home*, tells about a couple, Sue and Wilbur, who came for counseling. As they sat across the desk from the marriage counselor, Wilbur shifted nervously from one side of his chair to the other.

Sue sat stiffly with her arms folded defiantly and said, "I am not here because I want to be. My physician told me to come. I have an ulcer that is killing me, and he says it is not caused by any physical reason." As she spoke, she reached down into her shopping-bag-sized purse and pulled out an inch-thick manuscript—each page typed single-spaced on both sides. She slapped the document down on the desk and said, "That's why I am here!"

The counselor picked it up to see what it was. When he opened the manuscript, he saw a careful documentation of every slight, every hurt, every word, every deed that Wilbur had committed against his wife for the past thirteen years. (In subsequent visits, this proved to be a very accurate account of their married life.)

"That's what is giving me ulcers!" Sue explained.

The counselor said, "I want you to know, young lady, that it has been many years since I have met anyone" (Sue began to smile, and Wilbur slid further down in his seat) "as hostile and resentful as you are!" With that, Wilbur sat up a little straighter, and the counselor continued, "This is a record not only of the faults your husband has committed against you, but also of the sin you have committed against him, against God, and against your own body, for which you are now paying a price."

God's Word says that love "keeps no record of wrongs"

(1 Corinthians 13:5 NIV). You may be wondering how anyone could be so petty as to write down every slight done to them. Some people, however, have extraordinary memories and don't need a notebook to record hurtful incidents. They can cite places, dates, circumstances, and quote dialogue verbatim from years ago. Do you know someone like that? Do you live with that kind of person? Are you one of these I'll-never-forget people?

Sometimes our resentment comes out unexpectedly in little slips of the tongue: "You always...." Obviously, quite a memory tape is being played back in our minds. "Why, you never...." Never? That conclusion requires the amassing of a tremendous amount of data. Maybe we are not much different from that young lady with the manuscript after all.

Breakdowns in Communication

Another block to communication is a poor self-image. Many people who begin life with a low self-esteem have this image reinforced by others who criticize them, ignore them, make fun of them, and pooh-pooh their ideas. After a while they are convinced that they have nothing to offer; they are not worthwhile; nobody wants to hear what they have to say; and certainly no one cares how they feel. As a result, they learn to withhold their opinions, their ideas, and their personal feelings. This breakdown in communication affects all their relationships.

Do you contribute to a poor self-image in your spouse? Many husbands continually put their wives down by being sarcastic and uninterested in their ideas. Men who treat their wives this way will find themselves isolated from any form of meaningful communication.

Some wives destroy their husband's self-esteem by trying to usurp the leadership role in the home. She often snaps, "Are you a man or a mouse? Squeak up!" The last big decision she let him make was whether to wash or dry. A put-down is a good way to put off effective communication.

Adams also says that one of the most common blocks to communication is faultfinding. Instead of dealing with the problem in their marriage, a husband and wife will begin to attack each other. "If you wouldn't do this, it wouldn't be that way!" "Well, you think I am…." "What about the way you….?" "Yes, but you always…." The problem gets lost in the personal battle that ensues. Instead of focusing on the issue at hand, couples get sidetracked by resentment, hostility, and faultfinding.

Some people think the most important part of a discussion is fixing the blame on the guilty party. They think their calling in life is to be a Colombo or a Sherlock Holmes. Are you a blame fixer? Blame fixing destroys any possibility of creative problem solving. It is also a great and impassable barrier to good communication in a marriage. If couples would focus on the problem and not on each other's faults, they could find a solution to their marital difficulties.

Barking on the Inside

Communication can be blocked by two opposite, yet equally destructive, reactions—blowing up and clamming up. Some people do both.

The Bible says to "be ye angry, and sin not" (Ephesians 4:26). When a husband or wife blows up in anger, all sorts of vicious speech are spewed forth. He or she riles against his or her mate and tells him or her off in no uncertain terms. An explosion like that is definitely sin. Nothing brings communication to a halt quicker than the ranting and raving of an angry spouse.

On the other hand, some people have difficulty expressing their anger in any form. They close up like a clam, while their rage boils within them. Some husbands and wives suppress this kind of anger and resentment for years. This is probably why the apostle Paul said, "Let not the sun go down upon your wrath" (verse 26). If anger is dealt with on a daily basis, it will not have the opportunity to simmer inside and one day erupt into a violent explosion.

A story is told about a little girl who was walking down the street when a big dog came running toward her, barking ferociously. The girl froze, staring petrified at the big dog. Finally, a neighbor called to the dog, and the animal stopped barking. But the little girl remained standing very still. "It's all right, sweetie. The dog has stopped barking," the man said. The little girl did not reply. "It's all right now. The dog has stopped barking," he repeated. Finally, the little girl looked up and said, "Yes, but the bark is still on the inside."

Can you imagine the ferocious look on that dog's face? Has your spouse ever seen that expression on your face? Have you seen it on your spouse? Is the communication in your marriage frozen by the fear of a violent outburst? Maybe your mate has clammed up because the bark from your last argument is still ringing in his or her ears.

"Stop being mean, bad-tempered, and angry. Quarreling, harsh words, and dislike of others should have no place in your lives" (Ephesians 4:31 TLB). Destructive anger is sin. Confess it as such, and let Jesus Christ cleanse this area of your life. Then pray for your spouse to be healed of any emotional damage your "barking" may have caused.

Opening the Lines of Communication

If the level of communication in your marriage has broken down, Adams has a suggestion that is guaranteed to generate interest. He says your spouse will always be delighted to discuss how you have wronged him or her. If you can "confess your faults one to another, and pray one for another" (James 5:16), the lines of communication will be opened. Pride impedes honest sharing, but humility releases a flow of spontaneous give-and-take.

Write a love letter to your spouse this week. Concentrate on one single topic: your mate's good points. What do you appreciate about your husband or wife? Put your thoughts down on paper. Focus only on the positive side of his or her character—not the negative aspects.

You will be amazed at how this simple exercise will change your attitude. Then, as the way you perceive your mate is changed, the problems will begin to dissolve. In fact, many of them will disappear.

Communication is an art. We need to approach it the way we would learn to play the piano or the violin. Would you say, "Oh, I can't play the violin. I tried it once. In fact, I tried it several times, but it just didn't come naturally for me." Some people give up trying to communicate with their spouse because they tried for a while, and it didn't seem to work for them. Being a good communicator does not come naturally; it is a skill that must be learned and practiced.

If you are convinced that communication is the key to

success in your marriage, then keep on trying. Persevere in working toward developing a relationship of intimate sharing with your husband or wife. The rewards will far outweigh any amount of effort you have to put forth. A rich, fulfilling experience awaits you.

"Be completely humble and gentle; be patient, bearing with one another in love. Make every effort to keep the unity of the Spirit through the bond of peace" (Ephesians 4:2-3 NIV). True unity develops as husband and wife share their lives by communicating with one another. Communication must, first of all, be intellectual, then emotional and spiritual. Finally, it will be truly physical. The essence of marriage is communication.

Father, help us to tear down the barriers that prevent open and honest sharing in our marriage. Teach us to listen in love and speak the truth so that we can raise the level of communication between us. May our words and attitudes reflect the love we have in our hearts for You and for our mate. In Jesus' name. Amen.

Four

Sand In Your Shoes?

Marriage can be either tremendously constructive or unimaginably destructive to the lives of those involved. Let's look at what makes the difference between a constructive and a destructive marriage.

Nothing is more beautiful than two people when they are first in love! Both think they have met the most wonderful person in the world. If family or friends try to candidly point out any faults in your beloved, their words are coldly received. Certainly nothing worthy of notice could begin to compare with the overwhelming good that flows from this dear one. Ah, the wonderful astigmatism of romance. Love, indeed, is blind!

When you fell in love with your husband or wife, did you have such feelings about your beloved? Did you each share similar feelings with each other? Were you lifted right up out of this world into the heavenlies? At last you had found someone who could look beyond the braces and the blemishes and see you for the wonderful person you really are; someone finally had true insight into your real character. This constructive aspect of love was remarkable because—wonder of wonders—you began to improve and become the person your beloved thought you to be.

Wouldn't it be wonderful if this potential for constructive betterment continued into married life? All too often, however, something else begins to occur. To your utter amazement, you soon discover that your friends were right! He or she does have flaws. At first only the minutest ones are seen, and these can be overcome. But then things get worse—that big blob of toothpaste is constantly in the sink, the clothes are always left in the middle of the floor, and the door is never shut. As the little irritations begin to grow, it slowly dawns on you that, perhaps, you have been deceived—this person is not the man or woman you thought he or she was.

As you begin to concentrate on the negative aspects of your spouse's character, a shift in focus takes place. The lens is changed, and now the good points are all blurred. Instead, your husband or wife's glaring faults—the inconsiderateness, selfishness, and boorishness—all come into sharp focus.

Not only do you have this perception of your spouse, but you begin to convey to him or her how you feel. The principle that had worked to bring improvement when you were dating, now works in a destructive way: your spouse begins to become whatever you say he or she is— an ill-mannered oaf, a lazy bum, a fat slob. And soon, what you say is what you get!

Blinded by Criticism

Some years ago a man walked all the way from New York to California! At the end of his trek, reporters asked him if he had ever thought he wouldn't make it. "Many times," the man replied. When they asked what had almost defeated him, he answered, "Let me tell you. It wasn't the rushing traffic in the cities or the blaring horns and screeching brakes of cabs or trucks. It wasn't even those interminable Midwestern plains that just went on and on as if they would never end. Nor was it the ice-tipped mountains of the Rockies or the blazing sun over the desert. What almost defeated me over and over again was the sand in my shoes."

Although this unheralded, seldom-discussed irritant is never mentioned as the reason for divorce, "sand in the shoes" defeats many marriages. What is this irritating problem that erodes away the very foundation of a harmonious marital relationship? It is the abrasive sand of criticism.

Criticism poisons the atmosphere of the home. Husbands and wives are afraid to say anything different or do anything special, because a cutting word lies just beneath the surface, ready to lash out and cut them down. Marriage partners can no longer express love for their mate because of the rejection inherent in criticism. The bloom of love withers in an atmosphere of rejection, and divorce is often the result.

Faultfinding never accomplishes anything constructive. Criticism is sin, because the faultfinder is trying to play God. Jesus said, "Do not judge, or you too will be judged. For in the same way you judge others, you will be judged, and with the measure you use, it will be measured to you" (Matthew 7:1-2 NIV).

In the physical world, for every action there is an equal and opposite reaction. Jesus tells us that the same principle applies in the moral and spiritual realm. Yet we blindly continue on with our degrading and destructive criticism, not realizing that we are only making our own lives more and more miserable.

The next time you open your lips to find fault with your husband or wife, remember that you are condemning yourself. Criticism is always destructive—to both the person being criticized and the one doing the criticizing. It lashes out at the victim, but then recoils and strikes the criticizer in the back when he isn't looking.

Yes, ladies, you can get your husband to wipe his feet when he comes in the door. "I spent all day cleaning this room! Can't you ever remember to wipe your feet?" You can finally housebreak your husband and think you have gotten your point across. But in seventeen other ways you will receive your measure again, and you won't even know why it happened or where it came from.

One day you will say, "How could he have done that to me? What did I do? Where did I go wrong? How could he even have looked at her? I've been such a faithful wife."

You've been faithful, all right—you have faithfully pointed out every fault in your husband for twenty-five years! He's had enough sand in his shoes.

"What can he possibly see in her? She's older than I am and not as pretty!" But this other woman is probably a little smarter, because she can't even see his faults! She actually thinks there are some really nice things about him—and she tells him frequently.

When you criticize your spouse, you blind his or her eyes to your good points. The more faults you point out, the more of your faults your mate will discover, until neither of you can see anything good in each other. You don't treat anyone else this way. You don't condemn your friends. Yet you make the greater mistake of derogating the one on whom most of your happiness in this life depends, and you reap the harvest of misery. After counseling with some couples, I have concluded they must be Mr. and Mrs. Frankenstein, because both partners have painted a picture of some horrible monster.

All judgment proceeds from an attitude of pride; a proud person finds fault with others. Consider the Pharisee and the publican in the temple. The Pharisee said, "I thank You, Lord, that I am not like other men." What an implicit criticism of the whole human race! "I don't do this; I don't do that. I'm not like that publican over there at the other end of the temple." The publican, however, would not so much as lift up his eyes to heaven, but he smote his breast and cried, "God be merciful to me a sinner" (Luke 18:13). This man wasn't looking around finding fault with other people; he had a spirit of humility, and all he could see was his own sin.

This is what Jesus meant when He asked, "Why do you look at the speck of sawdust in your brother's eye and pay no attention to the plank in your own eye?" (Matthew 7:3 NIV). The plank in your eye is this unhealthy attitude of pride that judges and finds fault with others.

You say to your spouse, "Here, let me take that speck out of your eye," when a two-by-four beam is sticking out of your own. One has to be totally blind to the beam in his own eye before he can focus on the speck in another's eye. When a person comes under the conviction of the Holy Spirit, sees the sin in his own life, and says, "Woe is me, ...I am a man of unclean lips" (see Isaiah 6:5), he is not as likely to see the fault in his spouse's eye.

Goodfinding versus Faultfinding

Some of you are saying, "You mean I am never supposed to say anything critical about my husband or wife?" The Bible deals with that, too. We are told, "If a man be overtaken in a fault, ye which are spiritual, restore such an one in the spirit of meekness; considering thyself, lest thou also be tempted" (Galatians 6:1). Notice: it is a brother overtaken in a fault; it is not nitpicking at every little thing. That is the law of the jungle, where an animal is singled out by its predator and then later devoured by scavengers that pick and claw at its remains.

Some people suppose themselves to be spiritual because they can see the faults in others. They do not realize they are not acting like God; they are acting like the beasts of the jungle. God, in His infinite love, covers a multitude of sins. He looked down upon us in all our uncleanness, with all our faults, and sent His dearly beloved Son to die for us. God's way is the way of love, and "love covers over a multitude of sins" (1 Peter 4:8 NIV).

Instead of pointing out our faults to us, Jesus took them upon Himself on the Cross, bearing the burden of our guilt and the penalty for our sins. Christ is the friend of sinners—not the faultfinder of sinners. If we ask Him to forgive us of our sin, trusting in Him for salvation, Jesus accepts us as righteous. Acceptance—that is the purpose of redemption.

How can we who have been forgiven and accepted by a loving Savior turn around, criticize, and reject our spouse? If we want to love the way Jesus loves, we must strive to accept our husband or wife and overlook his or her faults.

How can you get rid of the sand of criticism in your marriage? How can you make the principle of "what you say is what you get" work in a constructive way? First of all, get rid of all resentment by forgiving your mate and asking him or her to forgive you for your sin of pride and criticism.

The next step is to determine that you will try to find the good points in your mate. God's Word tells us how to do this: "Whatever is true, whatever is noble, whatever is right, whatever is pure, whatever is lovely, whatever is admirable—if anything is excellent or praiseworthy— think about such things" (Philippians 4:8 NIV).

Think about the good things your spouse does. Take time to meditate on the positive aspects of your mate's character, and pray that God will give you eyes to see only good. Creatively consider what is good about your spouse. Pray about what caused you to marry your beloved. Every day share with your spouse something good. Instead of the same hackneyed, trite points you have managed to say before, express something new you have discovered about him or her.

The book of Proverbs tells us, "Withhold not good from them to whom it is due, when it is in the power of thine hand to do it" (Proverbs 3:27). The only way your husband or wife can know how you feel is for you to send clear and unambiguous signals that express your love. Don't withhold verbal expressions of your love; tell your spouse exactly how you feel about him or her. Everybody needs to know they have top priority in someone's affections.

A happy husband once said to his wife, "You reached into my life and found the good no one else had ever seen." A marriage can be destructive or constructive. Whether you see and share the faults or see and share the virtues is the determining factor. You can expect tremendous positive results when you begin to practice goodfinding instead of faultfinding.

Marriage at Its Best

One of the most practical formulas for strengthening husband/wife relationships was developed by Dr. Ed Wheat, a marriage counselor, physician, speaker, and author. In his book, *Love Life for Every Married Couple*, Dr. Wheat uses the acronym B-E-S-T to describe his method of improving the marital relationship: Blessing, Edifying, Sharing, Touching. We will deal with the importance of sharing and touching in later chapters, but the first two parts of this formula offer the antidote to faultfinding and criticism.

In the acrostic BEST, the "B" stands for blessing. In the New Testament, the word blessing comes from the Greek word *eulogia*, which simply means "to speak well of." Blessing our spouse means to speak well of him or her. It is the opposite of criticizing, nagging, or faultfinding.

First of all, blessing means that we will speak kindly to our husband or wife. We are to compliment and encourage him or her with our words. Encouragement and compliments tend to motivate people, stimulating them to do better. Criticism and faultfinding, however, are a depressant and tend to cause people to do less. By speaking well to our spouse, we can motivate him or her to improve in the weak areas.

Second, we need to speak well about our spouse. I am sometimes astonished by what husbands and wives say to one another and about one another in public. Some couples think snide remarks are clever or funny, but they pay the price for their comments in the privacy of their own home. How well do you speak of your spouse in front of other people?

Third, we need to express appreciation and thankfulness for what our spouse does. Unfortunately, this sometimes degenerates into a few simple things for which we are grateful. Some husbands view marriage as a kind of business arrangement. "I make the living. You keep the house and the kids. That's the deal. I do my part; you do yours. Who's to thank for what?" That attitude might make a good working arrangement, but it makes a lousy marriage. We need to be creative in showing appreciation and thankfulness, rather than simply applauding the same things over and over again.

Fourth, we need to pray regularly for God's blessings upon our spouse. We will pray for famine-stricken Ethiopia and the missionaries around the world, yet fail to pray regularly for God's blessing upon our spouse. Oh, yes, we pray for their health, we pray for their business success, we pray for their safety, but do we really pray God's richest blessing upon their innermost beings? We should pray that they would become all God would have them to be and that they would experience the fullness of joy God wants them to enjoy.

The "E" in Dr. Wheat's acrostic BEST is for edifying. Derived from the word edifice, it simply means "to build up." Instead of tearing each other down, we should be building one another up. We need to undergird our spouse and support him or her. You can help develop your husband or wife's self-image by building his or her confidence and encouraging your mate to become a well-balanced person. We often do this for our children, but fail to realize that our spouse has the same needs. Everyone has feelings of inadequacy, inferiority, weakness, and inability. When these are minimized by a spouse who emphasizes our strengths and talents, our self-esteem grows and makes it possible for us to do even greater things.

In Louis H. Evans' book, *Your Marriage: Duel or Duet?"* I found this poem by an unknown author. It describes perfectly how this principle of minimizing the bad and emphasizing the good works.

> I love you,
> Not only for what you are,
> But for what I am
> When I am with you.
>
> I love you,
> Not only for what
> You have made of yourself,
> But for what
> You are making of me.
>
> I love you,
> For the part of me
> That you bring out;
> I love you
> For putting your hand
> Into my heaped-up heart
> And passing over
> All the foolish, weak things
> That you can't help
> Dimly seeing there,
> And for drawing out
> Into the light
> All the beautiful belongings
> That no one else had looked

Quite far enough to find.

I love you because you
Are helping me to make
Of the lumber of my life
Not a tavern
But a temple;
Out of the works
Of my every day
Not a reproach
But a song....

I love you.

Begin today to shake the sand out of your marital shoes. Let the words of your mouth and the meditations of your heart be acceptable in God's sight. Then what you say will get you the kind of marriage you want.

Father, may we be a constructive force in the life of our spouse. Help us to be encouragers, uplifters, and goodfinders. Help us to know what it means to be truly spiritual and to be filled with love that covers a multitude of sins. For Jesus' sake, who thus loved us and clothed us with His righteousness. Amen.

Five

Making Marriage Work

Have you ever bought a new appliance, but couldn't figure out how to make it work? That is when you need to heed the advice of a poster I once saw, "When all else fails, read the instructions."

In America today, the institution of marriage is in serious trouble. In some states we now have each year an equal or larger number of divorces than marriages. In fact, Americans have achieved the worst record of marital failure in the history of mankind! What a tragic indictment.

You would suppose that any group of people who had experienced such obvious failure would be anxious to consult the Maker, read the instructions, ascertain the problem, and discover how to make marriage work. Yet that is not the case. Americans add one idiotic alteration after another to the mechanism of marriage—living together, open marriages, marriage contracts, communes. Then, when those twists in the machinery don't work, someone suggests abandoning marriage as an institution altogether.

America's approach to marital problems reminds me of an alcoholic whose drinking has brought him to the place where his boss has fired him, his money is all gone, his wife has left him, his home has been reclaimed, and his children hate him. At last, he decides to do something about the problem, so—he reaches for the bottle! "How stupid," you say. Yet many people think the answer to their marital problems is reaching for the divorce papers.

The Manufacturer's Instructions

Marriage for many couples becomes a battlefield that transforms their home into a literal hell on earth. David Engelsma, in his book, *Marriage: The Mystery of Christ and the Church*, puts it this way:

> In the world, marriage is the battlefield on which a vicious, relentless struggle rages between the tyrant-husband and the rebel-wife. Now the one, now the other is temporarily victorious. At present, in our society, the rebellious woman has the upper hand. If the world lasts, the male will again assert himself, overthrow the woman's dominance, and rule her more tyrannically than before. The Christian marriage is radically different. The husband rules in love. The wife submits in love. Marriage, thus, is not a framework for bitterest strife and mutual destruction, but a relationship of fellowship, joy, and mutual help. There is peace.

The biblical solution to the problem is to take the tyrant out of the husband and the rebel out of the wife. Peace! That is God's answer.

To reject God's solution is analogous to a tattered, dirty beggar from skid row questioning Rockefeller's principles of banking and economics. That would be ludicrous. For those of us who have proved such miserable failures in the area of marriage, to question God's formula for a peaceful home is more tragic than ludicrous.

Suppose we do decide to go back to the Manufacturer's instructions on how to make a marriage work.

Where do we find them? The fifth chapter of Ephesians contains some very interesting and controversial guidelines for the marriage relationship. Yet, as we read them, let us remember they are commands from God's Word.

> *Wives, submit yourselves unto your own husbands, as unto the Lord. For the husband is the head of the wife, even as Christ is the head of the Church: and he is the saviour of the body. Therefore as the Church is subject unto Christ, so let the wives be to their own husbands in every thing. Husbands, love your wives, even as Christ also loved the Church, and gave himself for it (Ephesians 5:22-25).*

A certain anxiety came over me as I faced this passage. I wished—for fear of being called a male chauvinist—that the apostle Paul had started with the instructions to the husband instead of the wife. To my surprise, I discovered I was not the only minister who shunned this topic. When I consulted Spurgeon, I found he skipped all the instructions given to the wife in this passage and dealt only with the husband. Criswell, in his excellent commentary on Ephesians, omitted this portion of chapter five altogether.

The apostle Paul, however, jumped right in without flinching. So I thought, "Well, Kennedy, you've never backed away from a challenge before, and you're not going to run from this one. You are going to deal with this subject head-on." And so I am!

Art Linkletter once read an interesting letter a little girl had written to God. "Dear God," she wrote, "are boys better than girls? I know that you are one, but try to be fair." Right from the beginning, let's understand that God is neither a boy nor a man. All concepts of human sexuality break down when we consider the infinite Spirit who is God. In the Gospel accounts, Jesus' treatment of women and His sensitivity to their needs portray the heart of God. Our heavenly Father has no favorites.

You may agree with that point, but then ask, "What about the apostle Paul? Everyone knows he didn't like women."

After preaching in a church in New York City, I got into a discussion about the apostle Paul with a young "liberated" woman. She could not understand how such a prejudiced man ever managed to get his writings included as part of Holy Scriptures. This revealed a great deal to me about her whole view of Christianity, the Bible, the inspiration and revelation of God, and the authority of God Himself as it is revealed in His Word.

If you believe that the Scriptures are the revelation of God, then you must accept the writings of Paul as inspired by the Holy Spirit. John Calvin said that we are to receive the words of Scripture as if they dripped from the lips of God. Remember, these are not my opinions, but clear declarations from the Word of God. If you disagree, you are not disagreeing with me or the apostle Paul; you are disagreeing with God, and your argument is not with me, but with Him.

Take Me to Your Leader

Two people riding a horse cannot both steer the same animal; someone must be the guide. You cannot go two ways at once. Two generals cannot supervise the same army; nor can two presidents manage the same bank. Only one person can be in authority. God's Word has a great deal to say about authorities and submission to them. A king's subjects must respect his authority; servants must be in subjection to their masters; children are to obey their parents; and wives are to submit to their husbands.

As I considered the various scriptural texts dealing with the wife's relationship to her husband, one central theme emerged. It is found not only in the passage from Ephesians, but frequently throughout the New Testament. See if you can discern what it is.

*Wives, **submit** yourselves unto your own husbands (Ephesians 5:22).*

*As the Church is **subject** unto Christ, so let the wives be to their own husbands in every thing (Ephesians 5:24).*

*Let...the wife see that she **reverence** her husband (Ephesians 5:33).*

*Wives, **submit** yourselves unto your own husbands, as it is fit in the Lord (Colossians 3:18).*

*Wives, **be in subjection** to your own husbands (1 Peter 3:1).*

*The holy women also, who trusted in God...**being in subjection** unto their own husbands: even as Sara obeyed Abraham, calling him lord (1 Peter 3:5).*

*The **head** of the woman is the man (1 Corinthians 11:3).*

What is the central theme of God's Word concerning the wife's relationship to her husband? Submission. The wife is commanded to be in submission to her husband. For some women that is a hard pill to swallow.

In this day and age, no one wants to be in submission to anyone. Rebellion is the order of the times; submission is out, and rebellion is in. The generation gap is simply children throwing off the authority of their parents. The feminist movement is the rebellion of wives against their husbands and other men in authority. "No man is going to tell me what to do!" One of the reasons for the widespread rebellion of children against parents stems from the rebellion of wives against the authority of their husbands.

While some reject the whole idea of submission, others try to redefine the teachings of Scripture and strive to make it mean something else. But the Greek verb *hupotasso* means "to submit" or "to be in subjection"; and the meaning is the same throughout the New Testament.

You might ask, "Why should the woman be in subjection? Why shouldn't the man submit to the woman and be in subjection to her?" In some homes, that is the way it is.

Suppose one Saturday a spaceship from Mars were to land in your backyard, and a little green creature were to crawl out. What would happen if he went over to your children and said, "Take me to your leader"? Where would they take him? Whom do your children consider the head of your house?

Who Made You Boss?

Have you ever been asked, "Who is the boss around here, anyway?" Whether it is you or someone else, one thing is for sure—someone has to be the boss. Our heavenly Father had some very good reasons for making the man, and not the woman, the boss. Let's look at why God placed the husband as head of the family

The most basic reason for the husband's authority is that God created man before woman and placed him in a state of preeminence in the Garden of Eden. "The head of every man is Christ; and the head of the woman is the man...forasmuch as he is the image and glory of God: but the woman is the glory of the man" (1 Corinthians 11:3, 7). Why is a woman not to usurp man's authority over her? Because "Adam was first formed, then Eve" (1 Timothy 2:12-13).

The feminist's opinion is that God created man, took one look at him and said, "Oh, I can do better than that"; so He made woman. This kind of rebellious attitude views God as some sort of bungler who knows nothing about the husband/wife relationship and didn't know how to make people in the first place.

God had a specific purpose in mind when He created woman. "The LORD God said, 'It is not good for the man to be alone. I will make a helper suitable for him'" (Genesis 2:18 NIV). The wife was not created to serve her own self-interests; she was created for her husband. "Neither was the man created for the woman; but the woman for the man" (1 Corinthians 11:9).

Modern women reject this fundamental virtue of the wife, claiming that she is an equal partner in marriage. They insist that marriage is a contract where no one is the final authority in the relationship—every decision is made by mutual agreement. The wife considers herself independent of her husband—with her own life, her own career, her own fulfillment as a woman, apart from her husband. Her main goal in life is not to be a helper for her husband, but to satisfy her own desires and achieve her own success. Such thinking is rebellion against the divine creation order of God.

In fact, this is exactly where Eve went wrong. God placed man as head of the marriage relationship because the woman had trouble following orders. "Adam was not the one deceived; it was the woman who was deceived and became a sinner" (1 Timothy 2:14 NIV). Because the woman was the first to sin, God told her, "Your desire will be for your husband, and he will rule over you" (Genesis 3:16 NIV).

Rebellion is still Satan's most effective temptation. It worked on Eve in the Garden, so he continues to use it on women today. Satan himself is the arch rebel who refused to be a creature subservient to God. When he rebelled against the divine creation order of God, the world was plunged into sin and chaos. A wife who rebels against God's order for the marriage relationship will throw her home and family into confusion and disorder. Woman's fallen nature is basically a rebel nature that must first be changed by the regenerating work of the Holy Spirit before she can even begin to submit to her husband.

How do wives rebel against the creation order God has established for the home? Some rebel openly, refusing to submit to their husbands in any way. Others ignore their husbands, go their own way, and live independent lives. They sleep in the same house, eat at the same table, but do their own thing. By refusing to be the helper to their husband that God created them to be, they are in rebellion against their Creator.

Some wives obey outwardly, but inwardly they are filled with bitterness and rebellion. They partially assent to submission by yielding themselves to meet the material and physical needs of their husbands. Like a maid or a servant, they take care of the home, the meals, and the children; but when it comes to inwardly yielding to being their husbands' helpmate, they rebel.

Submission is an inward attitude of heart that leads to obedience. Your adornment "should be that of your inner self, the unfading beauty of a gentle and quiet spirit, which is of great worth in God's sight. For this is the way the holy women of the past who put their hope in God used to make themselves beautiful. They were submissive to their own husbands" (1 Peter 3:4-5 NIV).

How Far Is Too Far?

Whenever headship in the husband/wife relationship is discussed, the question most often asked is, "Are there any limits to a wife's submission?" My answer to that question is based on the biblical concept of authority.

First of all, God's Word teaches that all authority is from God. No human being in and of himself has any authority at all. The only authority man has comes from God. The Bible also teaches that all human authority is limited to its proper sphere; no human authority has unlimited power. A parent has authority over his children, but he does not have the right to abuse them. No human authority can countermand the direct authority of God. A sergeant cannot override the orders of the general; the pupil cannot contradict the rules set down by the teacher. If any human authority endeavors to contradict God's commands, the Christian is bound by conscience to obey God rather than man.

What about an unbelieving husband? Is the wife to submit herself to him? Yes, unless the husband expects her to do something specifically forbidden by God, or if he forbids her to do something that God specifically commands her to do. When that happens, she should graciously, and in submission, do what God has said in His Word.

Submission is an attitude of the heart—whether the wife agrees with her husband or not. "Wives, in the same way be submissive to your husbands so that, if any of them do not believe the word, they may be won over without words by the behavior of their wives, when they see the purity and reverence of your lives" (1 Peter 3:1-2 NIV).

I read about a minister and his wife who enjoyed a beautiful relationship. A young seminarian had observed this couple on several occasions and noticed that the husband would do anything for his wife. The young man wondered about this until he came to live with their family while he attended seminary. Every afternoon, the wife disappeared for a while. Later, she emerged from her bedroom wearing a fresh dress, having her hair styled, and smelling of perfume—just in time to meet her husband at the door with a big hug and kiss. The young seminary student thought how wise this wife was. Her simple act of submission showed a deep respect and admiration for her husband that he reciprocated in many ways. This helped create the beautiful relationship they enjoyed together.

A wife who has a submissive heart will seek to please her husband because she loves and respects him. Her reward will be a devoted, affectionate spouse who will go out of his way to provide, protect, and care for her. Who could ask for anything more?

Heavenly Father, we want our homes to come under the rules of authority that You have established in Your Word. Help us, as husbands and wives, to submit to You and to one another in a way that is pleasing to You and in obedience to Your commands. In Jesus' name. Amen.

Six

Mistakes Husbands Often Make

After hearing a sermon on the husband/wife relationship, a couple told me what their little boy said as they were going to the car: "Gee, Dad, you've got the easy part. Mom has to submit to you, and all you have to do is love her."

It might seem that the Bible places the husband on a high pedestal of imperious sovereignty from which he looks down on his wife in her place of submission. But let's took at what God's Word actually says about this matter:

> Husbands, **love** your wives, even as Christ also loved the church, and gave himself for it....So ought men to **love** their wives as their own bodies. He that **loveth** his wife loveth himself. For no man ever yet hated his own flesh; but nourisheth and cherisheth it, even as the Lord the church....Nevertheless let every one of you in particular so **love** his wife even as himself (Ephesians 5:25, 28-29, 33).

That is quite a challenge—to love your wife the way Christ loves the Church; to give of yourself to your wife the way Jesus gave Himself for us. This is not an easy assignment, even for the bravest among us. Nothing less than absolute commitment and determination will enable any man to obey this command. In fact, without the power of the Holy Spirit, it is humanly impossible.

Problems occur when a husband reads this passage about his position of headship and starts thinking he is to exercise some form of harsh tyranny over his spouse. Having discovered that she is subject to him, he concludes that his will is sovereign and what he says goes! He begins to strut around the house like a little Caesar or Napoleon, ruling with despotic control over his family. Yet the apostle Paul said nothing about the husband controlling the wife; the command is to love her.

Some husbands abuse their position because they do not read how they are to be the head—as Christ is the head of the Church and the Savior of the body. Jesus Christ has infinite power and all authority, yet He lovingly leads us, not by pushing and shoving, but by showing us "a more excellent way" (1 Corinthians 12:31). Wisdom and restraint are the keys to loving, effective leadership. A husband who keeps his eyes on Jesus and acts according to His character will be blessed with a loyal, devoted wife who respects and admires him.

The purpose of headship is to keep the body out of trouble. As part of our human body, the head keeps the hand from burning itself and the foot from stepping on a nail. The command is to love your wife the way you love your own body—as much as you love yourself. Husbands, you are the head of your marriage relationship, and it is your responsibility to protect and care for your wife.

Some women nag their husbands and try to make them more loving. "If you loved me, you would do this and wouldn't do that." This kind of feminine manipulation is as much out of line as the husband who tries to terrorize his wife into submission.

Many husbands make the mistake of thinking they

must make their wives submit to them. But God's Word contains no such instruction. The wife must voluntarily submit, just as the Church voluntarily submits to the Lord. If your wife does not submit to you, that is not your problem—it is hers. She must answer to God for her rebellion.

While the wife is under the authority of the husband, the husband is also under authority. He must look to Jesus and seek God's will and direction for his family. When Christ is sovereign in a home, love reigns supreme.

Persons and Things

Have you ever thought about what the word "husband" really means? It comes from the words "house-band." The husband is a band that reaches around his house to protect it, hold it up, provide for it, and defend it from outside dangers.

One of the husband's main responsibilities is to provide for the financial and economic well-being of his household. For this reason, God created man with a physical and emotional makeup that enables him to go out and compete in the workplace. Unfortunately, in today's society, many men are failing in this basic responsibility, and more and more wives have to go out and get a job. Some women must work, but other women work because the husband is failing in his God-ordained duty to provide for his family,

When a mother has to work outside the home, the effect on the children—and the husband—can be devastating. Our society is already reaping the results of children who come home from school every day to an empty house. One of the main causes of delinquency among young people is the lack of stability and security that results when both parents work. A husband who forces his wife to work so they can have all the "extras" is actually robbing himself and his children of the "necessities."

At the opposite end of the spectrum are husbands who suppose that by providing things for their wives and children that they have fulfilled their obligation to love their family. A man who thinks this way may awake one morning to find that his wife is miserable and his children don't respect him. With righteous indignation, he cries, "What did I do to deserve this kind of treatment? Didn't I give them everything they wanted?" Yes, you did, but you failed to give them what they needed most: a personal relationship with you as husband and father.

One of the greatest causes of marital failure is the confusion over the difference between persons and things. We have trouble understanding that we are to love people and use things. In fact, things should be used to help us develop our relationships with those we love. Unfortunately, most of the people in this world love things and use people to get what they want.

Balance comes when we learn to put people before things and use things to help meet the needs of those we love. Husbands who have their priorities in order will work hard to provide for their wives and children without becoming workaholics who neglect their family relationships.

Women fall into this same trap. Because of the nesting instinct, their concern for the house and their responsibility to care for the children, they often fail to recognize what is most important—the people living in the home. Wives, do you want to know whether or not you put things before people? Then answer this question: Your husband walks in the door and leaves muddy footprints all over the just-waxed floor. How do you react? What is foremost in your mind? Your relationship with your husband or the kitchen floor? Wives who become fixated with things may one day find themselves left with a neatly cared-for, but empty, house.

Whom Do You Love?

Earlier, we discussed the independent wife who refuses to be a helper to her husband and seeks her own fulfillment apart from her mate. You husbands would be the first to say that she is out of God's divine order. But what about the husband who has his fishing buddies, his sports activities, and his hobbies and interests without giving any thought to his wife's needs? You know her—the golfer's lonely wife or the football widow.

I heard about a wife who had reached the limit of her frustration level near the end of football season. Her husband had been glued to the television every Saturday and Sunday, completely ignoring his wife. One weekend she had had enough. She planted herself in front of the television, stomped her foot, and said, "Now, I want to know, which do you love more, me or football?" After a long period of silence, her husband finally looked up at her, smiled feebly, and replied, "I love you more than hockey."

Although few men would admit they love football more than their wives, their actions display an independent lifestyle that says, "I don't need you." And that hurts.

Some husbands refer to Scripture for their defense. "But wasn't man created to be an independent creature? Wasn't the wife made as a helpmate for him?" Yes, the woman was made for man, but God gave her to him because man needed help! Man was not sufficient himself; he needed someone to help him and share his life. In fact, God said it wasn't good for man to be alone; independence was never part of the Creator's original purpose for marriage partners. The husband who lives his own life, stopping now and then at home to refuel, is defying God and declaring that it is good for man to be alone.

Ignoring your wife while you pursue your own pleasures shows a lack of respect for her. God's Word makes it very clear how a husband is to treat his wife. "Husbands, in the same way be considerate as you live with your wives, and treat them with respect as the weaker partner and as heirs with you of the gracious gift of life, so that nothing will hinder your prayers" (1 Peter 3:7 NIV).

How you treat your wife is a test of your Christian faith and your love for God.

> If anyone says, "I love God," yet hates his brother, he is a liar. For anyone who does not love his brother, whom he has seen, cannot love God, whom he has not seen. And he has given us this command: Whoever loves God must also love his brother (1 John 4:20-21 NIV).

We learned in an earlier chapter that love is doing and enduring. You show your wife that you love her by being polite, considerate, and attentive to her.

Making or Breaking Her Day

When you were engaged, you gave a lot of thought to how you could make your fiancée happy. You put a lot of creative energy into making her day with special treats and surprises. But now that you are married, other priorities have taken over—you have to go to work, you have your business to run, you have a home and cars to take care of, and you have to provide for your family.

Making your spouse's day is about 296th on your priority list—especially at seven o'clock in the morning. But the way you and your wife part from each other in the morning can make or break the day. Your leave-taking paints the hues on the background of both her mind and yours, predetermining the attitude with which you will return home in the evening. How do you exit from the house in the morning? This poem by Dr. Louis Evans sums up the importance of making leaving a positive experience.

> If I had known in the morning
> How wearily all the day
> The word unkind
> Would trouble my mind
> I said when you [or I] went away,
> I had been more careful, darling,
> Nor given you needless pain;
> But we vex our own
> With look and tone
> We might never take back again.
>
> For though in the quiet evening
> You may give me the kiss of peace,

Yet it might be
That never for me
The pain of the heart should cease.
How many go forth in the morning
That never come home at night,
And hearts have broken
For harsh words spoken
That sorrow can ne'er set right.

We have careful thoughts for the stranger
And smiles for the sometime guest.
But oft our own
The bitter tone,
Though we love our own the best.
Oh, lips with the curve impatient,
And bow with that look of scorn,
'Twere a cruel fate
Were the night too late
To undo the work of the morn.

Don't make the mistake of leaving your precious wife with cruel and unkind words ringing in her ears all day long. You never know when those may be the last words she ever hears you say.

Husbands make many mistakes, but most can be easily corrected by simply being more considerate and sensitive to your wife's needs. You would be surprised to find how little it takes to make her happy. Most men have a tendency to overlook the obvious, so try asking your wife for specific ways you can please her. It could change your marriage!

Most of all, don't forget that as you put the

Manufacturer's instructions to work in your marriage, it will become a smooth-running machine. When the tyrant-husband has been changed by Christ and replaced by a loving one, and the rebel-wife has been tamed by the Holy Spirit and given a submissive heart, joy and peace will fill your marriage and home.

Heavenly Father, by the power of Your sword-like Word in the hands of the Holy Spirit, change the tyrant-husbands and tame the rebel-wives. In their place raise up loving husbands and submissive wives who will love and respect one another. To the glory of Jesus Christ. Amen.

Seven

When You Are Going In Different Directions

While waiting in the Chicago train station, a young man was thrilled to meet and chat with a lovely young lady. A delight to behold and a pleasure to talk with, she captivated his attention. When the call for the train came over the loudspeaker, she stood. He immediately jumped up and said, "May I sit next to you on the train?"

She replied, "I'm sorry, but you can't."

Somewhat confused and feeling dejected, he asked, "Oh, you're traveling with someone?"

"No."

"Then why can't I sit next to you?"

She answered, "Because you're going to New York, and I'm going to California!"

It is difficult, if not impossible, for two people to develop a meaningful relationship when they're going in different directions. Our heavenly Father knew this, and He gave us these instructions through the apostle Paul:

> *Do not be [unequally] yoked together with unbelievers. For what do righteousness and wickedness have in common? Or what fellowship can light have with darkness? What harmony is there between Christ and Belial? What does a believer have in common with an unbeliever? What agreement is there between the temple of God*

and idols? (2 Corinthians 6:14–16 NIV).

A Christian man or woman should marry only another believer—not someone who merely claims to be a nominal Christian, but a genuine born-again believer who truly trusts in Christ as Savior. Those who disregard the injunctions of God's Word are disobeying His commands and will undoubtedly reap the pain and heartbreak that spiritual incompatibility in marriage always brings.

Sometimes spiritual incompatibility occurs after a couple is married—when one partner becomes a believer. Then we have the situation of a Christian living with a non-Christian. What is to be done? Sometimes the Christian will say, "Well, I should leave this man or woman because he or she is not a believer. I'm a Christian, committed to Christ, and I shouldn't live in this ungodly atmosphere."

The apostle Paul said no. If the unbelieving partner is willing to remain in the marriage, then the believer should not be the one to leave. "How do you know, wife, whether you will save your husband? Or, how do you know, husband, whether you will save your wife?" (1 Corinthians 7:16 NIV).

Cracking the Nut

If the Christian is not to leave, what should he or she do? The believing husband is to follow all the Bible's commands regarding loving his wife and treating her with consideration. (See 1 Peter 3:7.) That is enough to bring most women to the Lord.

On the other hand, a believing wife needs more

specific directions on how to win her unbelieving husband. The King James Version says the husbands will "be won by the conversation of the wives" (verse 1). Three hundred years ago, when this version of the Bible was translated, the word "conversation" meant your manner of life and had nothing to do with speaking. Unfortunately, many wives take this instruction at face value and do just the opposite of what the Bible says. A more modern version puts it this way: "Wives...be submissive to your husbands so that, if any of them do not believe the word, they may be won over without words by the behavior of their wives, when they see the purity and reverence of your lives" (1 Peter 3:1-2 NIV, emphasis added).

Sometimes a wife preaches at her unconverted husband night and day with one sermon after another. Then she complains, "My husband won't ever go to church!" No wonder. He hears it all day long from his own, personal unordained female preacher who has three points and a moral to go with anything she does!

Dr. C. S. Lovett has an interesting word of advice for anyone married to an unbeliever. In his book, *Unequally Yoked Wives*, he describes the "nutcracker technique." We are all familiar with a nutcracker. When a nut is placed between the handles and the pressure is applied, the nut is cracked. Dr. Lovett compares the two handles of the nutcracker to our works and our light. Jesus said, "Let your light so shine before men, that they may see your good works, and glorify your Father which is in heaven" (Matthew 5:16).

Dr. Lovett describes the woman who goes to church five times a week, reads her Bible every day, prays for hours, and puts Christ above everything else—particularly above her husband, to whom she is continually preaching. Her "light" looks and sounds more like fireworks. The submission and respect the Bible talks about is missing from her relationship with her husband.

Other Christian husbands and wives live godly lives, but they never tell their mate or anyone else why they are doing the things they are doing. Consequently, they have works but no light. Their works are wasted because they do not praise their Father in Heaven. The light isn't set forth to show that Christ is the source of the joy and peace in their lives. In order to be an effective witness in the home, good deeds must be accompanied by an acknowledgement of the reason for the "hope that is in you" (1 Peter 3:15).

The ideal is to have the works—the joyous, glad submission of the wife to her husband, or the considerate love of a believing husband for his wife—combined with the light. Let's see how this can be put into practice in a marriage.

A woman married to an unbeliever says, "My husband's always complaining because he can't stand instant coffee for breakfast. But I'm not going to get up in the middle of the night to perk coffee, when instant tastes just as good!" But what would happen if she did?

The next morning when her husband walks into the kitchen, he notices something different: the aroma of fresh-perked coffee! He looks down in amazement to find his coffee cup filled and waiting for him. The wife has done a good work.

Her husband says, "Hey, what's this? Fresh perked coffee?"

Now for the light. His wife says, "You know, dear, I've

been praying about our relationship as husband and wife. I know the Lord wants me to be a good wife to you. He wants me to please you, and I want to obey God's Word. I thought this was something you would enjoy, so from now on you will be having fresh-perked coffee."

The husband is squeezed between the wife's work and her light. Her husband is delighted, and Christ is glorified. Those of you with unbelieving spouses should try the "nutcracker technique." You might be amazed at the results.

How's Your Compatibility?

Someone gave me this definition of incompatibility: the husband provides the "income," and the wife provides the "patibility." Wouldn't it be wonderful if it were that easy? We all know that achieving compatibility between marriage partners requires effort and constant growth by both husband and wife. In addition to spiritual incompatibility, there are other areas where a husband and wife may not be in agreement.

One place where many couples experience incompatibility is in the bedroom. A judge who had heard divorce cases for over thirty years said that the underlying reason for the overwhelming majority of divorces was sexual incompatibility.

Millions of American women are experiencing little if any sexual satisfaction in their marriage. A female doctor said clinical studies show that from 40 to 50 percent of American women have some form of the hypoaesthetic syndrome, commonly called frigidity. Many wives are suffering from total sexual anesthesia: complete and total absence of any sexual feelings at all.

If you could sit behind a pastoral counseling desk and hear the anguish of husbands and wives trying to deal with this problem, you would know how serious it is. You would hear men say that they wake up in the night, look at their wives, and despise them. You would hear the sobs of brokenhearted women whose marriages have turned into an arid wasteland or a horrible nightmare.

Many people hold completely erroneous ideas concerning this matter of sexual relations and adjustment in marriage. One of the basic causes of frigidity results from the American woman's concept of the marital relationship and her role as a wife. She is barraged on every side by conflicting input regarding her identity as a woman and her need for fulfillment.

Modern society has confused the issue and forced women to find their identity outside the home. Their fulfillment no longer comes from being a homemaker and housewife, thus making wives feel insignificant and unnecessary. To fill the void, today's woman seeks status and equality with men in the working world.

The feminist movement tells her, "You've come a long way, baby. Assert yourself and enter into man's arena. You can compete with them because you are the superior sex." Many women have followed this advice and become the dominant personality in the marriage. In many cases, the wife has taken over as head of the home, having assumed the position of decision-maker and breadwinner. A woman who enters into competitiveness with her husband begins to view him as a threat. When this happens, the wife cannot respond to him sexually.

Clinical studies show that a female child reared in the

home of a dominant, masculine mother will, because of the attitudes toward men instilled in her mind and heart, be rendered frigid by the age of five. Many girls are taught that males are basically the enemy who seek to subjugate and dominate females. For this reason men must be competed with and regarded as animalistic beasts who take advantage of women for their own lustful pleasure. No wonder so many women today grow up with feelings of rejection, anger, guilt, and envy toward their brothers, fathers, and spouses. This attitude has produced in many women a complete inability to ever fully enter into their God-given birthright: the fulfillment of womanhood in the holy bonds of matrimony.

Sex—An Original Idea

In the past, women were taught that sexual desire was a male propensity and respectable women shouldn't exhibit any need for it. The Church has helped foster this teaching with legalistic dogma and man-made rules. Many women today suppose that sexuality is really a male characteristic—at least more so than a female characteristic.

In the last thirty years, an overwhelming amount of scientific study has been done in the area of sexuality. One incontestable proof has been brought to light: a woman in her normal state has as much sexual desire as any man.

This recent discovery by scientists and psychologists comes as no surprise to the One who created male and female. In the very first chapter of the Bible, we read that God made two sexes, not one: "Male and female He created them....God saw all that He had made, and it was very good" (Genesis 1:27, 31 NIV). The maleness of the man and the femaleness of the woman are good in God's sight.

God created sex. Some people have the idea that God made men and women, and the Devil came along later and pinned sex on them. Yet the very first thing God told people to do was to have sex—that was the first verbal commandment given to mankind. "God blessed them and said to them, 'Be fruitful and increase in number'" (v. 28 NIV). God is in favor of sex.

This principle was reinforced in the New Testament by the apostle Paul:

> *The husband should fulfill his marital duty to his wife, and likewise the wife to her husband. The wife's body does not belong to her alone but also to her husband. In the same way, the husband's body does not belong to him alone but also to his wife. Do not deprive each other except by mutual consent and for a time, so that you may devote yourselves to prayer. Then come together again so that Satan will not tempt you because of your lack of self-control (1 Corinthians 7:3-5 NIV).*

The only reason a married couple should not have sex on a regular basis should be an inspired burden to pray together about some specific need and for a mutually agreed period of time. When sex is neglected in a marriage, all kinds of problems can develop. The apostle Paul named one of them—lack of self-control that can foster temptation and lust beyond the God-designed realm of marriage. If husbands and wives would take these few verses seriously and fulfill their marital responsibility with an attitude of love and submission, Satan would not be able to create sexual incompatibility in their relationship.

Because of man's depraved nature, he has taken sex and twisted, distorted, and perverted it. Some people have exploited it for money, and others have made it shameful and disgraceful because of the way they have used it. The Bible makes it clear, however, that sex is not a shameful matter. Genesis tells us, "The man and his wife were both naked, and they felt no shame" (Genesis 2:25 NIV). Sex in its proper place is a beautiful and wonderful experience, not something to be embarrassed about.

The Bible says in Proverbs, "Rejoice in the wife of your youth.… May her breasts satisfy you always, may you ever be captivated by her love" (Proverbs 5:18-19 NIV). When the beauty and purity of sex are experienced as God intended—within the confines of the marital relationship—it produces the most profound satisfaction and the most meaningful human relationship known to man. God created this one-flesh relationship to be the height of ecstasy and physical intimacy, as well as the deepest expression of spiritual oneness between husband and wife.

A Different Approach

A man's sex drive, his potency, is essential to the perpetuation of the human race. Without it, mankind would cease to exist, and the earth would be depopulated in one generation. But the ability to enjoy sexual pleasure is absolutely unnecessary to a woman for the perpetuation of the human species. Dr. Marie Robinson, a medical doctor and psychoanalyst has made in-depth studies in this area of sexual frigidity. A woman may be, as Dr.

Robinson says, as frigid as a polar icecap, give birth to twenty-five children, hate every minute of it, and make her husband, herself, and her children miserable in the process.

Because her sexual pleasure is not essential to the continuance of the species, the sexuality of a woman is very delicate. Like a small tree planted with fragile roots, the winds of error and heresy can destroy that tree. This has happened to millions of women, leaving them deprived of their birthright, miserable in their marriages, and unfulfilled as women. The bitter harvest of this distortion in the American female is ghastly to behold. It has produced frustration, bitterness, dissatisfaction, discontent in the home and, in many cases, divorce.

Satan works in devious ways and attacks women where they are weakest. He likes to take advantage of this vulnerable area by psychological blockage of one sort or another to rob women of their sexuality. His evil purpose is not simply to make women miserable, but to destroy their relationship with their husbands—especially in marriages where the husband is not a Christian. Satan likes to produce a situation where a spiritless man and sexless woman live together in hell on earth. The result creates further rebellion in the husband against God and hypocrisy in the wife against the clear teaching of Scripture.

After years of trying to help women with this problem of frigidity, a Christian psychologist on the West Coast has been using a different approach. When he counsels women who say they are unable to enjoy sexual relations, his advice goes something like this:

You are refusing to accept God's statement that your femaleness is good and that your husband's sex drive is there for a purpose. What I want you to do is go home and repent. That's right! Repent of the heretical attitudes that you have had toward the Word of God. Repent of the distortions and denials of your sexuality. Stop striving to compete with your husband, and repent of the animosity that exists between you and the hostility that keeps you from yielding to him. Ask God to forgive you so you can experience the deepest and most profound oneness that God meant for your marriage.

This psychologist said he was amazed at the number of women who came back to report that their lives and marriages had been transformed after their hearts and minds were made right with God.

Ladies, if you want to be liberated, let me introduce to you the greatest Liberator of all times—Jesus Christ. He can set you free to be a woman in the highest sense of the word—to know why you were created, who you are, and how to experience the fullness of your birthright. He can forgive you of your sins and take away your feelings of inferiority and hostility. If you ask for His help, Jesus can enable you to experience the satisfaction, pleasure, and fulfillment that God intended for marriage partners to enjoy. Don't let Satan deceive you in this area.

What about you husbands? If I were to ask your wife, "How is your sex life?" what would she say? Are you approaching her with gentleness and an honest concern for her needs? Do you see sex as a holy, pure, and glorious expression of your love before God? Do you pray about this most important area of your marital responsibilities? Have you experienced the intimacy of soul and of body that God wants you to have—one flesh, one spirit, one mind?

Husbands need to realize that sex is a high and holy privilege that must be approached in a tender and compassionate way in order to experience the full rewards of the marriage relationship. Wives need to see clearly that they have been deceived by the Devil and robbed of what was inherently meant to be theirs by their Creator.

God's physical and spiritual ideal is for husband and wife to be one in a love relationship that leaves no room for competition, animosity, fear, guilt, or envy. If your marriage needs help, seek it and you will find it. Almost every case of sexual incompatibility can be cured. Often simply a helpful book or a skillful counselor can unlock doors that have long separated husbands and wives from the rich fulfillment that is their birthright.

Father, help us to experience the full extent of our birthright. May we come to know the blessings You have poured out upon us in Christ and all You have created for us to enjoy. We ask this in the name of Jesus Christ, our Lord. Amen.

Eight

Principles For A Successful Marriage

Love is friendship set to music." I like that, don't you? In a marriage, however, the orchestration sometimes turns sour, making the melody thin and strained. The harmony disappears and is replaced by a virtual cacophony of discord.

This was true of the angry wife who said to her henpecked husband, "Harry, are all men fools?" Meekly, he replied, "No, my dear, some are still bachelors." Not much music in that marriage! In fact, I would say that very little friendship exists between them. Like musicians who must spend years studying and practicing, marriage partners must exert a great deal of effort to make their relationship a symphony of love.

Many marriages need a tune-up. If we neglect our cars, they begin to chug and jerk until we finally realize that a tune-up is needed. Sometimes, however, more serious repairs are required.

Several years ago I purchased a shiny new Pontiac. Shortly thereafter, I parked it at Howard Johnson's, where I had gone for lunch. As I was leaving the restaurant, a policeman came up to me and said, "Is that your car over there?" He was pointing to a car about thirty feet from where I had parked. The car was facing in the opposite direction, and it was a wreck.

I replied, "No, sir, my car is new. It's over… It's… Well, I guess that is my car!" It seems that a lady looking for her car's brake had found the accelerator instead, leaped the curb, and done terminal damage to my new automobile. When I looked in the backseat and saw the hump that covers the drive shaft turned at a 45° angle to one of the back wheels, I knew my car had had it!

Perhaps you feel your marriage is like that car. Before you can work on tuning up the engine, you need to straighten out the framework. The rusted-out wrecks of many marriages litter the landscape, and those that still function often rattle and scrape along.

Suppose the government decided to put restrictions on owning a vehicle, and each family was allowed to purchase only one. You couldn't replace it or sell yours and buy another—that was the only car you would ever own. Do you think you would maintain that car any differently than you care for the one you presently own?

If you realize that your marriage is a permanent, once-and-for-all, indissoluble relationship that cannot be broken or replaced, would that make any difference to you? When we become convinced that marriage is a lifetime arrangement, we will cherish that relationship like a precious and prized possession, making sure it is constantly in tune and that every part is in good working order.

Raising Your Standards

We are deluged on every side with an avalanche of concepts and examples completely contrary to God's ideal for marriage. Television constantly beams them into our homes. From the Flintstones to the Honeymooners, we are given one example after another of how a marriage ought not to be. Stop and think about it. Almost every sitcom dealing with the family is a lesson in how to have an ungodly, unchristian marriage. If you look to the media, magazines, newspapers, radio, and TV—plus the examples of friends, family, and neighbors—your view of marriage will be warped and far removed from the standard that God expects.

A young man named Philip Henry fell in love and sought the hand of the daughter and heiress of Mr. Matthews of Broad Oak, England. The father, however, was skeptical, saying that although Philip was an excellent preacher and a fine gentleman, his ancestry was unknown. He told his daughter, "We do not know whence he came."

"True," his daughter replied, "but I know where he is going, and I would like to go with him." So they prevailed upon the father, and the marriage was consummated.

Twenty years later, Philip Henry wrote these words in his diary: "This day we have been married twenty years, in which time we have received of the Lord twenty thousand mercies—yet though we have been married so long, we have never been reconciled for there was never any occasion for it."

Can you say that about your marriage? To the extent that you cannot say those words—to that extent your marriage has fallen short of what God meant it to be.

Incidentally, the great Bible scholar, Matthew Henry, was an offspring of that loving relationship. It has been said that you cannot read Matthew Henry's works without getting on your knees, so close will he bring you to the throne of God.

I read about a couple celebrating their fiftieth wedding anniversary. When the husband was asked to say a few words, he made this comment, "Fifty years ago we came to the altar of God and were joined together in holy matrimony as one. We determined right then that every morning and night we would kneel beside our bed and pray together. We would pray with each other and for each other. In fifty years, not one harsh word or even one harsh look has passed between us." How many husbands and wives can say that about their marriage?

I believe God intended marriage to be a depth of communion, a height of fellowship, and a breadth of love beyond anything we have ever known in this world. We have cheated ourselves by accepting a third-rate concept of the marital relationship. It's time to expose the phony image the Devil has set before us—one that has produced untold misery in countless homes—and lift our eyes to God's elevated standard of marriage. You and your mate can become one in Christ.

Ultimate Oneness

Most of us have never even dimly seen or conceived what God meant a Christian marriage to be. Unless you have the power of Jesus Christ in your lives, I am convinced that your relationship can never be what God intended. Spiritual oneness of heart is absolutely necessary to a successful marriage. Without it, the true meaning of marriage will elude you.

God has designed marriage to be a oneness of mind, a oneness of emotions, a oneness of body, and a oneness of spirit. Unless these exist in your marriage, your relationship is out of tune and you are not "one flesh" as God purposed. Couples who consider sex the ultimate expression of oneness often feel dissatisfied because they try to have physical unity when no spiritual, emotional, or mental oneness has preceded it. The special unity between a husband and wife is more than a conjunction of bodies.

As long as a couple is divided at the very core of their beings—if the most important aspect of life is not shared as husband and wife—how can there ever be that deep communion of spirit and mind that makes two people truly one? Although they are living together as man and wife, they will invariably be going in two different directions and will never know marriage as God designed it.

People are like millstones. When a man and a woman get married, they bring a lot of rough edges to their wedding day. Before marriage, they had never been close enough to another millstone to rub off the coarse areas of their lives. But soon they begin to grind on each other—and it hurts. They squeal and yell, not realizing that God is working to perfect them. Many husbands and wives are quick to give up, and take their rough edges and run. But couples who allow the coarseness to be worn down and smoothed out are more likely to stick together and have a successful marriage.

Dr. Joseph Henry gives an excellent illustration of this in his book, *Fulfillment in Marriage*. He said that during World War II, two physics graduate students heard their professor say that someday a method would be devised for polishing glass that would replace steel as the flattest surface known to man. When this was done, he said, a revolution in technology would take place.

After graduation, these two young physicists formed a partnership and set out to prove their professor's theory. They established a laboratory and went to work. Several years later, after a very complicated process, they had a great breakthrough. They produced such a flat surface that it could be used to measure objects within two-millionths of an inch—a great improvement over anything previously developed.

When Dr. Henry visited their plant, one of the owners said to him, "See these two squares of glass? They have been put through this new process, and I want to show you something." Then he simply placed the two pieces together, handed them to Dr. Henry, and said, "Now take them apart." After he pulled, pushed, twisted, turned and exerted all of his strength, Dr. Henry still couldn't budge them.

The young physicist explained, "Two surfaces are held together by a certain number of points of contact, but ordinarily there are so few that they easily come apart. The points on these two pieces of glass, however, have been ground down until they are almost completely flat surfaces. They are held together by so many points of contact that it is almost impossible to get them apart."

If you let God rub down the rough edges in you and your spouse, nothing will be able to tear you apart. The grinding may hurt for a while, but I urge you to surrender to God's purpose in your life. The problem in marriage is always the same: sin. Like the points of a porcupine, sin keeps people apart. Sin always divides, and love always draws together. Only the love of Christ can rub away these pointed edges and smooth them down so that you can live in harmony with one another.

How To Increase Your Life Span

Did you know that married people live longer than single people? This fact was discovered in an analysis of insurance company mortality tables. A person who has never married or is divorced or widowed—regardless of age grouping, race, or sex—will have a shorter life span than a married person. Single people will also succumb more easily to a number of the most prevalent fatal diseases.

Maybe that's why God says, "It is not good that the man should be alone" (Genesis 2:18). Loneliness causes stress and predisposes people to disease and death. One of the most essential elements missing from the life of a single person is the touch of a loved one. In touching, we express our care and concern for others, letting them know they are loved. Warmth is communicated through a touch, and comfort is brought.

Jesus often touched people as He ministered to them. Today, psychologists and physicians are aware of the miraculous results that sensitive, affectionate touching can bring. Physicians say it removes distress and eases anxiety in a patient. The power of the touch heals not only the body, but also the soul. Touching a person calms their fears, lessens pain, and alleviates discouragement.

If touching is vital to our health and life span, no wonder God said a man should "cleave unto his wife: and they shall be one flesh" (Genesis 2:24). Cleaving implies the intimate, continuous kind of touching that creates oneness in the marriage relationship.

When I first began in the ministry, I decided to preach on verse 24 of Genesis 2. As a new preacher, I wanted to be very spiritual about this matter, and it bothered me that the Bible expressed cleaving in terms of the flesh. I thought, "Wouldn't it have been more spiritual if God had said 'and they shall be one spirit'"? Now that sounds better—one mind, one heart, one spirit.

But God said "one flesh," and, as usual, God is right. Unless a husband and wife experience intimate contact that involves touching, caressing, and caring, they will not be one spirit or one mind or one heart. Oneness begins with a touch.

Coming Unglued

Dr. Ed Wheat, a physician and marriage counselor who has authored several books, conducted a marriage seminar at our church. He made an interesting observation about teenagers involved in their first infatuation. When a young man and woman fall in love, they act like they are stuck together with superglue. You cannot keep them apart. When you see them driving down the street, it looks like only one person is in the car. No matter where they go, they are constantly holding hands. If their hands unclasp, their arms go around the shoulders.

Dating or engaged couples are always touching one another, and this creates that ecstatic feeling of romantic love. Then these love birds get married, and two years later you see them driving down the street with enough room between them to fit an elephant! Next thing you know, they are visiting a marriage counselor. "Pastor, it's just not there anymore. I don't feel the flutter; the romance is gone."

What happened? They came unglued. Now they

practically never hold hands, and it's been a year since he put his arm around her. About the only time they touch is when they have sex, and even that seems to have lost its glow.

Oneness without touching is impossible. The word cleave refers to a concept of gluing two pieces of wood together. You can put glue on both pieces, let them dry for the proper amount of time, but they won't stick together if they do not touch one another. Many marriages are being precariously held together by glue that has dried up and lost its adhesiveness. Couples must cleave if they are to be one.

Cleaving is different from the mechanical motion of petting Fido on the head and saying, "Nice dog, go away." That kind of touching should be reserved for those with fur and tails—not for a husband and wife who love one another.

I often hear wives say, "The only time he ever shows me any affection is when he wants sex." Mutually initiated nonsexual touching—caressing, hugging, sharing of life, one with another—is essential to a healthy marriage relationship. Some married people become preoccupied with sex because they are really seeking the warmth, reassurance, and affection that comes from intimate touching. Husbands and wives need sensitive caressing not necessarily related to sex, but involving the kind of affection that says to your spouse, "God has made you mine, and I will love you all my days."

A line from an old familiar song contains some good advice: "Hug him every morning and kiss him every night, for a good man, nowadays, is hard to find." That's even truer today. A good woman is equally hard to find, and she needs that special touch of affection from her husband. A married person who fails to receive affectionate touching from his or her mate can be just as lonely as someone who is single.

Rekindling the Romance

How about your marriage? Do you and your spouse have the same intimate oneness that existed when you were dating? Compare the amount of touching you did then to the amount that you now experience. Are you cleaving the way God says you should? Or are you and your mate like two plastic bubbles rolling around the house, occasionally bumping into one another as you go your separate ways, with no cleaving, no oneness, and no feeling of intimacy?

Many people have a warped idea of love and marriage. They think you fall in love, get engaged, and a wonderful feeling of romantic love fills your heart. Then you get married, and the romantic love gradually fades away over the next few years as you go about raising children, making a household, earning a living, and so on. But Dr. Wheat says that is not God's plan at all. God expects the feeling of romantic love, excitement, and ecstasy to grow throughout marriage.

How can you keep that feeling of love and romance alive in your relationship with your husband or wife? Dr. Wheat says, "Nothing can build or rebuild an intense feeling of love in a marriage as responsive touching, reaching out to a responding partner."

The renewal of love begins with a decision of the will that says, "I will reach out, as Jesus did, to touch and heal and restore my marriage." The action of reaching out to your spouse expresses your love in a way nothing else can. Dr. Wheat says, "The more freely you express your affection in physical terms of touching and pleasuring the other, the more love you will 'feel' for your marriage partner."

I cannot overemphasize the importance of sensitive, affectionate touching, but I can include what Dr. Wheat tells married couples who read his book, *Love Life for Every Married Couple*: "If you practice everything else in this book, but do not touch each other frequently and lovingly, the thrill of romantic love will be absent from your marriage." Don't miss out on this God-given blessing.

Developing Spiritual Unity

Although your marriage may never be perfect, you can achieve far beyond what most people ever dream is possible. That high and lofty ideal of marriage—one man and one woman joined together for life in a holy, indissoluble, intimate relationship of oneness—should be the goal set before you and your mate.

Spiritual unity is the key to oneness in marriage. The closer you draw to Jesus—the One who breaks down the barriers of sin that separate and divide—the closer you will draw to one another. The farther you move away from Jesus, the greater the gap between you and your mate.

Maintaining that personal relationship with Jesus Christ requires spending time talking with Him in prayer—and in listening to His voice as He speaks to you from God's Word. As your faith and trust in God are developed, you will become more sensitive to your mate and better able to meet his or her needs. When both spouses know Jesus Christ as Savior, they share a spiritual unity that binds them together in love the way nothing else can.

The basic principle of a successful marriage is love. "For God so loved, He gave…." (See John 3:16.) Love is giving of yourself to your spouse and desiring to put his or her needs before your own. Love requires a conscious effort to please your husband or wife and make his or her life as happy, pleasant, and peaceful as you possibly can. Open yourself to Jesus Christ—the source of all love—and ask Him to come into your heart and fill you with His love.

God in Jesus Christ has not only given us marriage as a high and holy ideal; but, by the power of His Word and His Holy Spirit, He has also given us the strength to reach for that ideal.

Acres of Diamonds

In the book, *Acres of Diamonds*, Russell H. Conwell recalls the story of a prosperous Persian man who left his family and sold his property to go in search of diamonds. His search, however, was in vain, ending in poverty and death. But the farmer who had bought his land found acres of diamonds lying in the fields behind the house. This discovery unearthed some of the world's largest diamonds and produced one of the most magnificent diamond mines in history. The treasure sought by the first man had belonged to him all along; he just never knew it.

What do you see when you look into your backyard? The Bible tells us that the true treasure of life can be found in relationships—with God and with people. God has placed us in families so we can discover in our earthly relationships something of that special treasure found only in heaven above.

If you want to discover the hidden "diamonds" in your marriage relationship, you must possess two qualities. First, you must have perseverance—don't give up even when it looks like you've found worms instead of jewels. Second, mutual effort must be exercised by both partners. It is unrealistic to think you will discover anything if you let your husband or wife do all the digging while you lean comfortably on your shovel. Get in there and get your hands dirty; dig down and pull out the ugliness by the roots.

Failure to live according to God's high standard for marriage is to sin against the instructions of God's Word. If you willfully refuse to make an effort to improve your marital relationship, you deprive yourself and your spouse of one of the greatest sources of joy in this world. And you deny your children the best gift you can give them—a happy father and mother.

What is your marriage like: disastrous? so-so? or terrific? May God grant you the desire and priority in your life to apply God's principles to your relationship with your husband or wife. Decide today that you are going to discover the treasure that had been hidden from you: those "acres of diamonds" right in your own backyard.

Father, may the Holy Spirit work to soften our hearts toward one another so that we can realize our own sinfulness and determine to show Your love to our mate. Forgive us for the many sins, slights, and selfishness that keep us apart as husband and wife. Grant us a new view of marriage—the oneness that Christ alone can give. May His Spirit of love fill our hearts and help us to experience the depth of oneness and the height of communion that You desire for us to know. We pray that Jesus Christ may be glorified in our marriage relationship. In His name. Amen.

Let me pray for you and your marriage.

Heavenly Father, send Your Holy Spirit to move in the hearts of the husbands and wives reading this book. Cause them to be committed to the principles of marriage found in Your Word. May the communion of their lives enjoy the richness of the promises of God. In Jesus' name. Amen.

Save Our Nation

Nine

The Importance Of Marriage

*Therefore shall a man leave his father and
his mother, and shall cleave unto his wife:
and they shall be one flesh.*

—Genesis 2:24

Before the state, before the Church, God created the oldest institution on this planet, and that is the institution of marriage. It is the oldest and the most universal of all of God's institutions. Wherever you go in this world today, whatever continent, whatever nation, you will find that men and women are joined together in the bonds of matrimony and are rearing families.

Today I want to talk to you about the importance of marriage at a very critical time in the life of marriage. It is remarkable that in the entire history of the human race, what has happened in just the last few years—a millisecond in the history of mankind—is a massive effort to destroy that institution. Even more remarkable is that this effort is making ominously large strides forward.

But as far as the biblical record is concerned, God created one man for one woman. So it was in the beginning. It is really awesome to think, gentlemen, that God took a part of a man and tailor-made woman for him. We were made for each other by divine design. So it was seen in the

Old Testament, and also the New.

Christ performed His first miracle at a wedding in Cana of Galilee. When Christ was asked about the departures in the Old Testament concerning some who had taken numbers of wives, He said that was because of the hardness of their hearts. But it was not so from the beginning, and He brought them back to the very creation of the human race and what God has done. Marriage is of historical and biblical importance, and it is basic and essential to the culture in which we live.

This nation has been built upon good families. That has also been the strength of every nation. Even Napoleon Bonaparte said that what was needed was good mothers …women in families rearing children, and with that France would be strong. He was a very perceptive man. It is important for culture, it is important for the individuals, it is important for the husbands, and it is important for the wives.

No-Fault Assault on Marriage

Marriage has been under a three-fold assault in the last few decades like it has never seen before. There was the no-fault assault, where lawyers (politicians) decided they were just going to make it easier to get a divorce. The result was the skyrocketing divorce rate in America. One recent sociologist said that there are mountains of evidence that show that there never was a law passed that brought so much misery and unhappiness to so many people as no-fault divorce. Some of you have probably been through that. It has been, indeed, tragic.

I have talked to many people who have told me, "We just don't love each other any more. Things have gotten so bad we can't go on. We just have to get a divorce. After all, didn't we get married just to be happy?" With that self-centered, self-indulgent view of hedonism, as we find prevalent today, it seems a perfectly logical thing to get divorced. "I am not happy now. If I get a divorce, I am going to be happy in the future."

Like all of the lies of Satan, time generally proves them to be false. What have the studies shown? There have been more sociological studies on marriage and divorce and families in the last few decades than ever before. They have shown that couples who were at the point of getting a divorce and were about to throw in the towel, five years later, of those who went ahead with the divorce, 22 percent were happy. Of those who decided to stick it out, seek help and counseling and try to fix their marriage (which for most seemed probably hopeless), five years later, 80 percent said they were happy. God's way is the right way. Unfortunately, only too often we discover that too late.

Studies have shown that married couples, more than divorced or single people, are generally happier and have more wealth; they, on average, have better homes; they feel their lives are more fulfilling; (note this) and they have more fulfilling sex lives than single people—in spite of what is portrayed on many TV programs on the air. No. God's way is always the right way.

Children

Of course, when asked, "What about the children?" we were told by the no-fault divorce people, "They will bounce back." They are just sort of like basketballs. They bounce back. What have the studies shown? Sociological studies have shown that the children of divorce do worse in school. They drop out more, they make worse grades, they get into more trouble.

Keep in mind, these are averages, and I am not trying to put a guilt trip on anyone. Some of you may have been divorced when you had no power to do anything about it. You were deserted, abandoned, or whatever, and you are doing the best you can to rear your children. Some of you are doing an outstanding job but, on average, children drop out of school more, make worse grades, and get into more trouble. They are expelled from school more often, they are more likely to take drugs, they are more likely to drink alcohol more frequently, and they commit more crimes while still in school. No, that is not a very high bounce, is it?

Then, in life itself, they don't do as well either. On average, they commit more crime later, they make less money, and they are more unhappy, and though they despise divorce, they are more likely to get one than those that have lived in intact families.

You may remember a longitudinal study that was begun about eighty or ninety years ago in California by Dr. Terman. He examined the lives of fifteen hundred children for their entire lifetimes. It was an eighty-year, longitudinal study. You say, "That must have been a very old doctor." Yes. He died long before the study was over. Other doctors picked it up. These young people called themselves "Termites," after his name.

What were the results? Again, some of these fifteen hundred children, came from broken homes; others came from intact homes. The one thing they discovered was that on average, children of broken homes lived four years less. You want to get a divorce? On average, you are hacking four years off the life of your children. Some say, "It's a personal matter between your mother and me and nothing to do with you." Yes, it has something very definitely to do with you. It's going to shorten your life, on average.

Indeed, it is very important for children. The basic reason for marriage was that men and women might not only have their own lives fulfilled and strengthened, and might grow in grace together, but also, they would provide a safe and healthy place to rear children in this world.

Feminist Assault

There is not only the no-fault assault, but then there was the Feminist assault upon marriage. You remember that, don't you? The Feminists said that marriage was a jail cell, a prison for women, and so they abandoned it. They said it was a terrible thing for women, and all of their fulfillment in life was going to depend on their not getting married.

As you may recall, several of the leaders and founders of that movement lived long enough to say that the movement was a great failure. Many of these women were rushing, as the biological clock was ticking, to get married and to have children. They found that as important as a spread sheet might have been in their business, babies loved back and accounting sheets did not. The Feminist movement was a disastrous attack, a failed effort.

Homosexual Assault

The most current one is the homosexual assault on marriage. This is more serious than any before it, because here they are trying to destroy the very institution of marriage—they are trying to redefine marriage. Throughout the entire history of the world, marriage has been a union between one man and one woman. President Bush said in a declaration that marriage is a union between one man and one woman. He hoped it would be that way, and efforts were being made to protect it.

Marriage is in great need of protection. Ten years ago, there was not a single nation in the world that allowed anything other than a union between a man and a woman. There are some people that just can't be married to other people. You can't marry your sister or your mother or your daughter. You can't marry the household pet. There are some things you just can't do. Always it has been so that marriage is a union between a man and a woman. That is the way God designed it in the beginning.

What has happened? Today there are three countries that allow marriages between two men or two women. The first was the Netherlands, and then Belgium, and now, more recently, Canada.

And in our own country the Supreme Court of Massachusetts recently ruled that the State Legislature there must rewrite state law to make same-sex marriage legal and it won't end there. Already the homosexuals, through their legal arms, have instituted suits on all 37 of the states in America which have passed DOMA laws—the Defense of Marriage Acts. They plan to take them to court. They are using small groups of unelected officials in the courts to overthrow an institution which has existed as long as mankind has existed—and they have been amazingly successful.

What does a homosexual marriage look like? The longest term we have to take a look at it is in the Netherlands. One sociologist made a study and found that the average marriage between two men lasts 1.5 years. Furthermore, during that time, men have eight or more other sexual partners per year in that one and a half years. That would mean that during the time of that "marriage," this man has had an adulterous relationship with many other men. That is not something they would like to have known, but that is the fact.

In the United States, studies show that 75 percent of heterosexual married couples report being faithful to their vows. Again, from our media you would not suppose that it would be five percent, much less 75 percent!

It is interesting. What is it that the homosexuals want? Is it just that they want to get married? No. A number of their leaders have said that they don't really want to get married. All of the legal entanglement that that involves is something that would take away their freedom, which is the essence of their whole lives. The idea of "until death do you part," and monogamous relationships is utterly abominable to them.

Then, what do they want? They have said what they want is to destroy marriage altogether. They don't want to become like us, as so many naïve people think. What they want to do is make us like them, and open the door to all kinds of sexual chaos. If two men can get married, what about three or five? That is called polyamory, and many loves and group marriage and all such things as this are already in the wings and waiting to be filed in our courts. It would produce absolute cultural chaos in this country. Mother and father, husband and wife would be old-fashioned in a generation. This nation would be unrecognizable. This is the most dangerous attack on marriage the world has ever seen.

What Can Be Done?

What can be done? It appears that the courts cannot be counted on to act responsibly. Even the DOMAs, the Defense of Marriage Acts, which are passed by nearly 40 state legislatures, are vulnerable. You may recall the decision by the Supreme Court to overturn the case in Texas, where the law there was that sodomy was a crime. That law was passed by the legislature of Texas. It was overturned by the Supreme Court with the stroke of a pen. It is believed that would be true of all of the DOMA acts, so that marriage would not be protected in any state in the union.

What can be done? The experts say the only thing that can be done is a constitutional amendment. The U.S. Congress is considering a Federal Marriage Protection Amendment, which says, in effect: Marriage in the United States of America is a union between a man and a woman.

Passing a constitutional amendment is a very difficult thing but not passing this one would be disastrous. I hope that you will pray about it. You will certainly be hearing more about it. We have been working with all kinds of other Christian organizations to do what we can to help pass the Federal Marriage Protection Amendment, and we will yet do more. You need to first pray about it. That is vitally important. I hope you will make marriage in America a regular matter of prayer. Second, contact your congressman and senators and tell them that you want the Federal Marriage Protection Amendment passed, because marriage is too important to be destroyed in America. We all need to work to strengthen our own marriages, which have been weakened by the various other two assaults I mentioned before—the no-fault, the Feminists, and now the homosexual assault on marriage.

Marriage is vitally important. It was obviously felt to be so by God, who made it the first institution He created, and that with His own hands. We need in our day to defend it as best that we can.

Heavenly Father, we are grieved at the lengths to which ungodly people will go to attack the basic institutions and virtues and principles upon which this nation was built. We ask, Lord, that you will cause their efforts to come to naught. Help us to be faithful to pray that our Congress may act, that the states may confirm the Federal Marriage Amendment solidifying marriage as a union between a man and a woman. We ask all of this in the powerful name of Jesus Christ. Amen.

Ten

Turning The Tide

Town and Country magazine once made a study of the presidents of one hundred top corporations in America. What did they find? A picture of swinging executives shuffling from one wife to another, always looking for a new model? No! They found that these successful, corporate presidents had a divorce rate of only 5 percent. The study concluded that perhaps marriage might not be that bad after all. In fact, it may even contribute to one's success.

Few people would argue against the benefits of marriage. Even those who get divorced have a tendency to marry again. What we have in America today differs little from the pagan polygamy that exists in some uncivilized parts of the world. In our modern society, however, serial polygamy is practiced—a man may have many wives, or a woman may have many husbands—they just have them one at a time.

The Futurist magazine said that if the present trend continues, divorce will soon be the manner in which most marriages end. The final result of getting married will be getting divorced. What a tragic prediction! Should we, as Christian husbands and wives, be concerned about this current trend?

Edward Gibbon, in his monumental work, *The Decline and Fall of the Roman Empire*, said that one of the principal reasons for the dissolution of Rome was the prior dissolution of the families within it. From the time Romulus and Remus established that city on the seven hills, there was only one divorce in its five-hundred-year history.

Then the law was changed, and divorce became more accessible and more acceptable in the eyes of Roman society. As families began to crumble, the foundation of the Roman Empire gave way. Before long, hordes of barbarians swept down from the north; and Rome, weakened and corrupt from within, fell to her enemies.

After the Pilgrim population reached 70,000 in this country, there were six divorces over the next seventeen years—one-third of one divorce per year. During the colonial period, the divorce rate worsened, with one divorce out of every five hundred marriages. By 1812, one out of every 110 marriages ended in divorce.

One author, writing during World War II, said the alarming increase in the number of divorces in America brought on by the war would have serious effects on our society in the future. When he made that statement, there were relatively few divorces by today's standards. During the 1940s, the total number of divorces was in the tens of thousands. By 1959, the author's worst fears had come to pass with 395,000 divorces that year. In 1961, there was one divorce for every 3.7 marriages, and by 1979, the number had climbed to 1.8 million divorces a year. Today, in California, there is one divorce for every marriage.

If Rome fell when the family was dissolved, what do we in America have to took forward to?

Whose Business Is It Anyway?

A young couple came to Dr. Louis Evans some years ago and said, "Well, Dr. Evans, we think our marriage might go on the rocks, but after all, that is definitely our business." Millions of people today would echo that same sentiment—that divorce is a private matter and not the business of the Church, the society, or the nation. But is it? Is divorce merely a personal matter? Dr. Evans' reply to that couple was, "Your marriage is everybody's business!"

In his book, *Your Marriage: Duel or Duet?*, Dr. Evans says, "Marriage is a nation's business." A great pier that juts out into the midst of the ocean is pounded relentlessly by huge waves. If one piling of that pier gives way, one after another will soon crumble until the entire pier finally collapses into the angry waters. According to Dr. Evans, the same principle holds true for marriage and society. A nation is only as strong as the individual marriages and families on which it is built.

Three hundred years ago Jonathan Edwards, a dynamic Calvinistic preacher, was largely responsible for the Great Awakening in this country. His famous sermon, *Sinners in the Hands of an Angry God,* brought thousands of people to Christ. Edwards was also the most original and outstanding philosopher America ever produced. His father was one of the founders of Yale University.

Jonathan Edwards married a godly woman, and over the past three hundred years his descendants have included the following: 265 college graduates, 12 college presidents, 65 university professors, 60 physicians, 100 clergymen, 75 army officers, 80 prominent authors, 100 lawyers, 30 judges, 80 public officials, 3 Congressmen,

2 United States Senators, and 1 Vice President of the United States.

Sociologists have compared the effects of Jonathan Edwards' life and marriage to another man living at the same time: Max Juke—a derelict and ungodly vagabond who married a woman of similar character. Over the generations, their union produced the following: 300 children who died in infancy, 310 professional paupers, 440 crippled by disease, 50 prostitutes, 60 thieves, 7 murderers, and 53 assorted criminals of other varieties.

How can anyone conclude that the quality of a marriage is a personal matter? Every marriage and every family, in one way or another, affects the strength of our nation.

At least 50 percent of all children born this year will see their parents divorced, adding a significant number to the millions of children who already come from broken homes. Psychologists tell us that the disintegration of a child's personality can almost always be traced back to the breakup of the home. Personality disintegration in a child can later lead to alcoholism, delinquency, and crime. In our nation, an overwhelming number of violent crimes are committed by young people. Whose business is that?

Divorce affects not only society, but the Church as well. When one couple in a church gets divorced, others are immediately infected, and they begin to think, "If the problems in our marriage get too tough, we can always get a divorce like Mr. and Mrs. So-and-so."

Every divorce within the Church family weakens the entire Church as a moral force in the nation. Its example is sullied, the power of its influence is reduced, and its opportunities to reconcile men to Christ are diminished.

Divorce then moves far beyond the personal to affect the nation, the Church, and the eternal destiny of thousands of people.

Just a Piece of Paper?

Someone said to me recently, "Marriage is nothing but a piece of paper." This kind of attitude lowers marriage to the level of a business agreement that can be cancelled any time the two partners change their minds. No wonder the divorce rate is so high in our country. "I take thee to be my lawfully wedded wife, as long as it feels good." Many people repeat the marriage vows, but 50 percent of them really mean "'til divorce us do part."

Our society has been called the "me generation," seeking mainly the gratification of one's own desires and pleasures. This kind of thinking is the ultimate expression of humanism and the total denial of the teachings of Christ.

Marriage, however, cannot withstand the "me" philosophy. *Current Trends* magazine said, "The search for self-gratification is inconsistent with the commitment and discipline involved in building a permanent marriage."

Dr. Kinsey, after talking to thousands of people, said that the number one element necessary for a successful marriage was a determination and commitment to make the relationship succeed.

Marriage, as an institution, was ordained by God and created before the Church was established or before governments were formed. Because God ordained marriage, it cannot be dissolved by man. Jesus said, "What therefore God hath joined together, let not man put asunder" (Matthew 19:6). The Bible makes it clear that there are only two grounds for divorce: one is adultery, and the other is the irremediable desertion of a believer by an unsaved partner.

A judge in New York City once gave these instructions to jurors who were deciding a divorce case: "Ladies and gentlemen of the jury, you should clearly understand that we have nothing to do with the religious or sacramental aspects of this marriage. We are only dealing with the laws of the State of New York. These people are bound together by God, and that bond is not to be touched by what we do here today. They will be as married in the sight of God when we finish our work as they were before we began. And many people fail to understand that fact."

In Malachi 2:16, we read God's opinion on the matter: "'I hate divorce,' says the LORD God of Israel." Every time a couple decides to get a divorce, they should receive a letter saying, "I hate divorce," and signed: "Jehovah, God and Judge of the universe before whom every man and woman will one day stand."

Innumerable books have been written on the subject of divorce. Classes have discussed the problem, and counseling sessions have tried to get to the heart of the matter. But too often these futile attempts have been like the ambulance that arrives after the car has gone off the road and crashed on the rocks below. Instead of being among the ambulances and hearses at the bottom of the cliff, let's try to build a safety rail around the road at the top and help prevent the tragedy of divorce.

God's Safeguard

God created and ordained marriage, but He did not leave it without safeguards. To protect and guard the sanctity of the highest earthly relationship man can know—the one between husband and wife—God gave a specific commandment: "Thou shalt not commit adultery" (Exodus 20:14). This eighth of the Ten Commandments was given to purify and protect the procreation of life.

The command is simple, unqualified, irrevocable, and negative: "Thou shalt not commit adultery." No reason is given, as in some of the other commandments. So destructive and damning is the sin involved that no argument is necessary. Since marriage is the most basic of human relationships from which all others—the family, the Church, the state—are built upon, it is essential that the husband/wife relationship be jealously guarded from every form of attack.

In His teachings recorded in the Gospels, Jesus hits hard at the source of the problem, taking His commands beyond law. "You have heard that it was said, 'Do not commit adultery.' But I tell you that anyone who looks at a woman lustfully has already committed adultery with her in her heart" (Matthew 5:27-28 NIV). The lustful look—the sin of the heart—is condemned because "out of the heart come evil thoughts…adultery, sexual immorality…" (Matthew 15:19 NIV). No wonder the Bible tells us to guard our hearts and our minds.

I am amazed at the attitude of professing Christians and how lightly they regard this extremely dangerous sin of lust. In this land, overrun with pornographic magazines, books, and motion pictures, it is vital for everyone, especially young people, to avoid the snare of lust and to flee, as the Scripture says. (See 2 Timothy 2:22.) Most women see this as a male problem, but immodest women contribute to the lust of men by the clothes they wear.

Sexual immorality is a particularly serious sin. All other sins are outside of ourselves, but the Scripture says, "He who sins sexually sins against his own body" (1 Corinthians 6:18 NIV). For this reason, immorality damages the human spirit and produces traumatic consequences for the individuals involved.

The tragedy of adultery is that it also affects others. It is a sin against the other spouse and breaks the conjugal vows made before God and men: "Forsaking all others, I choose thee." It is also a sin against the children, creating half-orphans who are denied the security of growing up in a home with both a father and a mother.

Not only is adultery a sin against the individual, the other spouse, and the children, it is primarily a sin against God. When a Christian commits adultery, he joins Christ—who lives within—to a harlot. (See 1 Corinthians 6:15.)

God will not tolerate immorality, and the consequences of His anger are eternal. "The works of the flesh are manifest, which are these; adultery, fornication, uncleanness, lasciviousness…. They which do such things shall not inherit the kingdom of God" (Galatians 5:19, 21).

In the Old Testament, when a person transgressed a law of God, they were instructed to bring certain sacrifices to obtain God's forgiveness. There were two sins, however, for which no sacrifice—and no forgiveness—was stipulated: murder and adultery. The penalty was death. In the New Testament, through Jesus Christ, we can find forgiveness of sins for which, under the Mosaic law, there was no forgiveness.

Identifying the Problem

What actually causes divorce? Psychological problems? Incompatibility? The wrong genes? What is the real problem? Most people don't like to talk about it, but the Bible makes it very clear. The reason for divorce is sin.

Jesus said that the law allowed the Israelites to put away their wives because of the hardness of their hearts. (See Matthew 19:8.) Hardness of heart is a direct result of sin.

Some of you, having heard the Word of God, know that you are guilty of adultery, immorality, lust, and uncleanness. You know you are living in sin.

Most of you, however, have been faithful to your spouse, but other sins are destroying your marriage. The sin of selfishness is a real marriage-killer. How about the sin of criticism, anger, and unresolved hostility? Being unloving, unappreciative, impatient, unkind, or the sin of seeking your own instead of your mate's well-being—all these sins drive husbands and wives apart.

Sin causes divorce, but the Good News is this: Sin can be forgiven. God loves you, and He wants to free you from the bondage and heartache of sin. Get alone with God and His Word and let the Holy Spirit speak to you concerning the hidden sin in your life. If you acknowledge your sin and repent of it, Jesus Christ, by His shed blood will cleanse you and forgive you of your sin. (See 1 John 1:7–9.)

God wants you to live an abundant, fulfilling life.

With the help of the Holy Spirit, you can live victoriously over the sins of the flesh.

Committed to Change

"Okay, I won't get a divorce," you may say. "But what about my spouse? He (or she) will never change. I guess I'll just grin and bear it."

You may be able to bear it, but one thing you won't do is grin. This kind of attitude denies the very reason Jesus Christ died for our sin—so that God, by His Spirit, can change us and make us more like His Son. Receiving forgiveness for your sin is only the beginning of healing for your marriage. Although sin is the basic cause of divorce, repentance and forgiveness must be followed by a firm commitment to improve the marriage relationship.

In order to prevent divorce, our concept of marriage needs to be revamped. We need to understand that marriage is a holy relationship, chosen by Christ to represent the relationship between Himself and His Church. Because marriage was ordained by God, His blessing on that union is absolutely essential. Without God at work in a marriage, it will not succeed.

Although one in every two married couples ends up divorced, certain categories of marriages have a much higher success rate. A national survey revealed that when two criteria are present—the couple attends church, and they pray together at home—there was only one divorce in one thousand marriages. Sounds like pretty good odds to me!

Many marriages fail because husbands and wives forget the importance of having God in the center of their relationship. The simple basics of praying together, reading and sharing God's Word, and attending church as a family are left out of their marriage. If you try to build a marriage around each other, around the children, or around some common interest, it will disintegrate. A successful marriage must be built on Jesus Christ.

Before the problems in your marriage can be solved, you need to commit yourselves to the task of improving your relationship. You need to say to one another, "Come what may, we are going to work out our problems and stay together." Unless you are determined to work through to a solution, change will never take place.

Every marriage needs change; there is no perfect marriage. Constant growth reflects a healthy relationship. Commit yourselves to developing oneness by sharing your lives—talk openly with one another, do things as a couple, and spend time alone together. If you make a determined effort to do these things, you will be surprised at the change that will take place in your relationship.

You and your spouse may not be able to change yourselves, but God can change you. By His grace and the power of His Spirit, God can take cold hearts and confused minds and forge them in the "one" He ordained when He created male and female.

We can turn the tide of divorce—one marriage at a time.

O God, some reading this book are ensnared by the sins of sexual immorality and are helpless in their bondage. Lord, set them free. May shackles be broken as they come to the Cross to be cleansed by the blood of the Lamb and to be made new by the power of Your Spirit. Help them to walk in freedom through

Jesus Christ. Father, by the power of Your Spirit, change us and make us more like Jesus. Even as Christ is one with the Church in that mystical union, may we be committed to being one with our wives and husbands in that sacred institution of marriage. We invite You, O Lord, into our relationship to make it all You intended it to be. In Jesus' name. Amen.

Eleven

Reasons To Reject Same-Sex Marriage

The wisest man to walk the planet—someone who shaped Western civilization—explained marriage some 2,000 years ago. Maybe it's worth knowing what he said.

"Have you not read," Christ said, "that He who made them at the beginning 'made them male and female,' and said, 'For this reason a man shall leave his father and mother and be joined to his wife, and the two shall become one flesh.'"

Here we have the short answer as to why marriage is always the union of a man and a woman and never the union of two men or two women. The Creator said so—and He makes the rules. He designed the different but complementary physical, emotional, and mental, characteristics of men and women that are the stuff of which marriages are made. *Vive la difference!*

For those with ears to hear, God and our nature shout the same message about marriage: "It's a man and a woman for life." But for those who dismiss God and nature (not recommended) here are a few more reasons why same-sex marriage is a cultural catastrophe in the making.

Harm to Children

First reason: Harm to children. Social science research strongly supports the common-sense observation that children do best when raised by their married mother and father. The thirteen family scholars who surveyed thousands of studies for the *Why Marriage Matters* report, reached the conclusion that "marriage is an important social good associated with an impressively broad array of positive outcomes for children and adults alike." Children raised by their married parents are less likely to experience child poverty, commit suicide, commit crimes, suffer physical or sexual child abuse, or to divorce later in life.

So when Rosie O'Donnell's then six-year-old son told her, "I want to have a daddy," he was pleading not just for what he wants, but for what he needs. Rosie's response, shared on ABC's *Primetime Thursday*, was to tell her son, "If you were to have a daddy you wouldn't have me as a mommy, because I'm the kind of mommy who wants another mommy." So much for putting children first.

Three decades into America's epidemic of fatherlessness, we know that depriving children of fathers damages them and their future. Same-sex marriage will rob children of what they need most: the love and nurture of both a mother and a father.

Second reason: The decline and fall of marriage. Hoover Institution researcher Stanley Kurtz has documented how 10 years of same-sex marriage, or its functional equivalent, civil unions, in Denmark, Norway, and Sweden has led to far fewer marriages and rocketing illegitimacy. Kurtz reports that a majority of children are born out of wedlock in Sweden and Norway. In Denmark, some 60 percent of first-born children do not have a married mother and father. That's bad news for children, since unmarried parents are much more likely to split up.

"Marriage in Scandinavia is in deep decline, with children shouldering the burden of rising rates of family dissolution," writes Kurtz. "And the mainspring of the decline—an increasingly sharp separation between marriage and parenthood—can be linked to gay marriage."

Over the Horizon

Third reason: Polygamy and more. Once it is established that two men have the right to marry, it will be impossible to deny that same right to others. If marriage can be redefined as any two men or two women in love, what rational principle precludes extending that logic to polygamy—or any other combination of emotionally attached men, women, or children? If emotional attachment is the only standard by which we judge fitness to marry, then no sexual arrangement is off the table.

Family law theorists are pushing in this direction. Kurtz cites, among many examples, University of Michigan law professor David Chambers, who thinks homosexual marriage will help to soften society to other alternatives. "By ceasing to conceive of marriage as a partnership composed of one person of each sex," Chambers wrote, "the state may become more receptive to units of three or more." The ACLU, which has announced its support for removing laws against polygamy, will be glad to help.

Fourth reason: Say good-bye to free speech. It's speak now or be forced to forever hold your peace, if same-sex marriage is legalized nationwide. That sounds extreme, but the push to silence dissent is already evident in Canada, where homosexual marriage has now become legal.

In addition, the Canadian parliament has passed a measure criminalizing "hate speech" against homosexuals. The law has a religious exemption, but that is little comfort, since a Saskatchewan court has already found the Bible to be hate literature. It upheld in 2003 a fine against a man who placed a newspaper ad with Bible verses on homosexuality. Also last year, Swedish authorities arrested a pastor for "hate speech against homosexuals" after he preached a sermon with biblical references to homosexuality.

Take your pick. The short answer or the long answer. God and nature, or a parade of bad outcomes that will follow the state's stamp of approval on same-sex marriage. Forty years after the sexual revolution promised "free love" and brought divorce, illegitimacy, STDs, fatherlessness, and abortion, the last thing our nation needs is one more misguided social experiment.

All this is why Congress must pass the Federal Marriage Amendment. It must act to protect marriage from activist courts eager to impose, against our will, a radical redefinition of marriage in America. If Congress does not act, there is little doubt that very soon, the U.S. Supreme Court will.

High Court and Homosexual Marriage

The High Court has already tipped its hand on this matter. In throwing out a Texas statute forbidding sodomy, a 6-3 majority ruled in 2003 that "our laws and tradition afford constitutional protection to personal decisions relating to marriage, procreation, contraception, family relationships, child rearing, and education." Then, after citing the relevant text from its 1992 ruling in *Casey v.*

Planned Parenthood, the Court announced that, quote, "Persons in a homosexual relationship may seek autonomy for these purposes, just as heterosexual persons do."

And while the Court sought in *Lawrence v. Texas* to deny the obvious conclusion that it was opening the door to homosexual marriage, Justice Scalia knew better. "Do not believe it," he said in dissent. Likewise, the Massachusetts Supreme Judicial Court also knew better. That court cited *Lawrence* in reaching its radical conclusion that the Bay state must allow homosexual marriage.

Whatever courts may say, the American people are lining up to say no to homosexual marriage. Eighteen states have now passed state constitutional amendments limiting marriage to a man and a woman. We, the people, have begun to pull the plug on the homosexual marriage movement. Popular support for true marriage is also evident in the more than 450,000 people who joined our Center for Reclaiming America's "Stand for Marriage" petition campaign in 2004.

But so long as federal courts remain poised to unite men in matrimony, state action alone will not safeguard the institution of marriage. We must erect a constitutional firewall now to protect marriage, to protect children, and, ultimately, to protect the social order.

"He who made them at the beginning 'made them male and female.'" It's still true. And however much they may wish it, activist courts cannot rewrite the law of nature inscribed into our very DNA. Marriage is not malleable. If we seek to remake it, we will break it.